TRANS MISSION

MY QUEST TO A BEARD

Little, Brown and Company
Hachette Book Group
1290 Avenue of the Americas, New York, NY 10104
Visit us at LBYR.com

Originally published in 2017 by Wren & Rook in Great Britain.
First U.S. Hardcover Edition: May 2019
First U.S. Trade Paperback Edition: May 2020

Little, Brown and Company is a division of Hachette Book Group, Inc. The Little, Brown name and logo are trademarks of Hachette Book Group, Inc.

The publisher is not responsible for websites (or their content) that are not owned by the publisher.

The Library of Congress has cataloged the hardcover edition as follows:
Names: Bertie, Alex, 1995– author.
Title: Trans mission : my quest to a beard / Alex Bertie.
Description: First U.S. edition. | New York : Little, Brown and Company, 2019. | "Originally published in 2017 by Wren & Rook in Great Britain"— Title verso. | Audience: Ages 12 and up.
Identifiers: LCCN 2018039547| ISBN 9780316529037 (hardcover) | ISBN 9780316490337 (ebook) | ISBN 9780316490344 (library edition ebook)
Subjects: LCSH: Bertie, Alex, 1995– | Transgender people—Great Britain—Biography—Juvenile literature. | Transgender youth—Great Britain—Biography—Juvenile literature. | Transgender people—Identity—Juvenile literature.
Classification: LCC HQ77.8 .B47 2019 | DDC 306.76/80941—dc23
LC record available at https://lccn.loc.gov/2018039547

ISBNs: 978-0-316-49032-0 (pbk.), 978-0-316-49033-7 (ebook)

Printed in the United States of America

LSC-C

10 9 8 7 6 5 4 3 2 1

TRANS MISSION

MY QUEST TO A BEARD

Alex Bertie

LITTLE, BROWN AND COMPANY

NEW YORK BOSTON

CONTENTS

Five years ago, I left a note on my dad's desk.

Dad,

Last Christmas, I wrote Mum a letter—and I know you read it too, but we never spoke about it and since then that's all I've wanted. I just want to be honest and I really need your support because...well, you're my dad. I guess I'm just scared. Scared of talking to you, scared of what you'll think of me...just scared of everything.

The letter to Mum was basically about my gender and how I was questioning. It's been like this for three years, and every day it gets harder to live with myself while having this massive problem hanging over my head. The black and white of it is that I feel male. Mentally I see myself as male. I've never felt female and everything about being a girl just makes me cringe and hurt. Hearing people say she, *Birth name,* her, daughter, girls...It just makes me so uncomfortable and I genuinely find it hard to respond.

I'm in a lot of pain living in this body. I find the idea of swimming daunting, meeting new people is a huge fear, I don't have the confidence to apply for a job, my period is a monthly reminder that my body doesn't match who I am inside, and I can't even bear the thought of going out in public with my own family in case someone mistakes me for a boy. I wish I had been born physically male so that I would never have had to write this stupid letter. I feel humiliated and like a disgrace to our family.

This is definitely not something that happened overnight; it's been like this for so long. Like I said, for the past three years I've been trying to come to terms with it myself. At first I accepted the fact that I was still young and that my feelings could change, but now I know what I want and I can't see my future any other way.

I can understand if this is hard for you, and I realize that this will be difficult for everyone—but trust me, I wouldn't choose feeling this way if I could. I also know that this isn't something that can be sorted out right away. It's all pretty medical-based, a lot of which can't even happen until I'm eighteen. I just don't want you to worry and I want you to know that I'm well aware of everything that comes with this and the effect it could have on my future.

We don't have to talk about it right away and I don't expect anything to change overnight; I just wanted you to know.

Alex

INTRODUCTION

It's like someone has Frankensteined my head onto a hideous alien body.

I'm not good at first impressions, but screw it: here we go. My name's Alex Bertie. I like pugs, doughnuts, and retro video games. I have tattoos, I make YouTube videos, and I sleep with my socks on.

I'm also transgender. Yeah, that's usually the part that throws people. I was categorized as a girl at birth and identified as female until I was fifteen, when I finally realized I was a transgender man. That makes it sound like I suddenly had some light bulb moment, though. In reality, coming to grips with my identity meant years of confusion and self-hate, both before I came out as trans and after. In order to make myself feel more comfortable in my body, I decided to transition from female to male. This was a physical process (such as seeking hormone replacement and having surgery) and also a social one (I told my friends and family, and changed my name, for example).

The center of all my problems as a trans person is body dysphoria. It's the whole reason I needed to transition. Dysphoria is the feeling that the body I was born with does not match the gender identity in my head. Everyone has different triggers for dysphoria, but the main ones for me were my chest, genitalia, lack of body hair, high voice, face/body shape, and hearing my old name, just to name a few. If you've never experienced dysphoria, you might think, "Hey, nobody's 100 percent happy with their body—can't you just deal with it? Why are you being so dramatic?" But dysphoria is so much more than disliking a part of my body. It's this unbearable feeling of self-hate in the back of my brain at all times, which I desperately try to suppress and pacify. Sometimes it's fine, safely tucked away in a corner of my mind. Then something triggers it and it punches me in the face. Suddenly all I can think about is this thing about myself that isn't right.

At times, I have felt repulsed by my own skin.

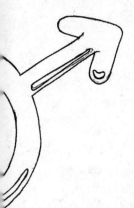

And that's the problem: it's my own skin. I can't get out of it, I'm stuck there.

I realize that may sound depressing and dark, but I assure you my story is also full of some delightful and pretty ridiculous memories. I'd like to show you that while I've faced some difficult challenges, I'm now the happiest I've ever been. While I can't get out of my skin, I have been able to make some big changes. Over the last six years, I've told my family and friends about my trans identity, changed my name, battled the health care system, started taking male hormones, and had surgery on my chest. It hasn't been an easy ride, but to wake up now feeling more comfortable with my body is a true blessing. I'd be lying if I said that my transliness (sometimes you just need a noun for being trans; I've chosen to use "transliness") wasn't a huge deal or that it didn't matter, because that one segment of my identity has played a huge part in shaping who I am as a person. It's also become a more public part of me than I ever imagined. Throughout all these years of self-discovery, I've been uploading videos about my life to YouTube. My channel has gained a bigger following than I ever imagined, and it's become my passion to share my transition story. Nothing will ever beat the feeling I get when I'm approached by someone saying my videos have helped them.

But other than the surreal YouTube life I experience once in a while, I'm just a regular dude working a nine-to-five job, trying to live my life as happily as possible.

I'm not really a writer, but I have had some different experiences that I'd really like the world to know about. It's the information you won't find on TV shows or in news articles about trans people—it's the real stuff. The emotions, the practicalities, the self-doubt… the stuff they can't cram into sixty minutes and that doesn't create a provocative headline. This is the first time I've ever put out my story from start to finish, and I've done it because I felt it was really important for there to be a book about a transgender man's true experiences.

1

LET'S GET SOME THINGS STRAIGHT

Your gender is how you feel in your head, as opposed to what's between your legs.

I wanted to explain the difference between sex, identity, and expression right away because I feel like knowing these things brings you a little closer to understanding why not every person born with a penis is a man or why not everyone born with a vagina is a woman. I'm not a professional, so I can't guarantee that this is going to be 100 percent accurate, but I'll try to make it short, useful, and understandable!

Biological sex
This is how the doctors categorize you when you pop out of the womb. Based on science and anatomy, it depends on which sex organs (both internal and external) you have at birth. A person born with a penis is labeled male, and a person with a vagina is labeled female.

So male and female: that's it, right? Nope—intersex is a thing! It wouldn't be right if I didn't mention intersex identities here. Intersex describes a person who doesn't fit into either "male" or "female" definitions of biological sex. An intersex person might be born with sex organs that are more ambiguous, such as an enlarged clitoris, no vaginal opening, or a split scrotum. The list of variations is endless. It's not all external—some people live their whole lives not knowing they have internal organs that don't correspond with their outer organs. In most countries, a doctor basically chooses the person's biological sex based on how "typically male" or "typically female" their sexual organs, hormones, and chromosomes are when this situation arises. However, some countries, such as Germany, have an intersex option on birth certificates so people are not incorrectly categorized as definitively male or female. That matters, because the biological sex you are assigned at birth plays a huge role in how most people are raised.

Gender identity
Gender identity is different than biological sex. Your gender is how you feel in your head, as opposed to what's between your legs. That means your gender identity can be different from your biological sex. For example, my biological sex is female, whereas my gender identity is that I'm a man. That's why I'm described as transgender. On the flipside, someone whose biological sex is female and their gender identity is female is known as "cisgender." That's easy, right? Good!

Gender is a social construct—that is, the concept is created by humans and defined based on our social and cultural differences. Humans have divided genders by actions, appearances, mannerisms, interests, and so on. In Western culture, we tend to think that men are strong, blunt, and aggressive, whereas women are sensitive, thoughtful, and shy. These rigid, "traditional" stereotypes encourage people

In recent years, people have begun to think of gender as more of a spectrum.

to believe that there are only two gender identities: male and female. That is the gender binary. But if you look around today's society, people are breaking out of those stereotypes all the time. In recent years, people have begun to think of gender as more of a spectrum, with people not just falling on the "male" or "female" ends, but everywhere in between—and sometimes, nowhere on the spectrum at all.

Gender expression

Your gender expression is how you present yourself to other people, regardless of your biological sex or gender identity. It's the way you act, dress, and so on. For a lot of people, their gender expression goes hand in hand with their gender identity, but I have some friends who dress in a very feminine way but feel their gender is more neutral. That's totally okay, because they're just doing what feels right for them. As a society, I think we're taking big steps toward not caring how people express their genders: maybe one day, hair will just be hair and clothes will just be clothes, without assumptions of gender being attached to them.

My gender expression has always been very stereotypically masculine, but that wasn't a conscious choice when I was growing up. I didn't want to "dress like a boy"—they were just the clothes I felt comfortable in. Over time, as I became more aware of my gender identity, I steered clear of feminine clothes because they made me feel dysphoric. Not everyone gets the choice of having a "fuck it" attitude when it comes to what they wear or how they act. But everybody does get the choice to be respectful. If it's not hurting anybody, what's the issue?

Dudes wearing makeup or ladies not shaving their legs isn't going to kill anybody.

Sexual orientation

This is who you're attracted to, and it's completely separate from gender identity. We've all heard the words gay, bisexual, and lesbian, but sexual orientations don't stop there. There are all sorts of terms describing different preferences. For example, I identify as pansexual, which is pretty close to bisexual, but isn't about being attracted to only men and women. I can be attracted to anybody, regardless of where they fall on the gender spectrum. Other sexualities include being asexual (lacking sexual attraction to others) and demisexual (where the person doesn't feel a sexual attraction unless there's an emotional attraction there too), just to name a few. Take a look at the glossary at the back of the book for more!

When I first transitioned to male, people would get a little confused about my sexuality and even theirs. Once, my best guy friend (who's actually straight) looked at me with confusion on his face and said to me completely out of the blue, "So...if we got together...would that be straight or gay?"

A huge belly laugh escaped from me before I could reply. "It would be pretty gay, mate. I'm a guy and you're a guy."

He started to respond, "But scientifically, you—"

I cut him off before he could finish, because I knew he was trying to talk about my genitals. I'm a man, and two men getting together is gay—it's as simple as that. After a lighthearted lecture, my friend eventually got it.

Being trans has definitely tested my temper at times. I've had to hone the ability to look past questions that seem offensive to find the genuine curiosity behind them. A lot of the time, people don't realize what they're asking is rude, so I've had to become an expert at answering difficult questions while keeping my cool—but still letting the questioner know that they've hit on a touchy subject.

Okay, so after that primer, the basics are down. Let's jump in!

2

CHILDHOOD

As kids,
nobody cared
about who you
were or what
you wore.

I guess we should start at the beginning. I was born on November 2, 1995 in the south of England. The doctors in the hospital took one look at my genitals and slapped an *F* on my birth certificate. *F* for female, not fail—though that would actually have been kind of appropriate given the present circumstances.

My earliest memories are of watching my dad play Nintendo 64 in our small apartment, waiting for my mum to get home from work. My dad introduced me to video games at a really young age with Mario and Sonic the Hedgehog, until eventually I graduated to *Grand Theft Auto* when I was about nine. It's probably not ideal for a nine-year-old to play games where they murder people, but luckily I don't think I picked up on the more mature references in the game. Unless it was a scary game that would keep me up at night, I was usually allowed to play it.

At the time I was too young to notice, but the area I lived in until I was five was not a nice place. I can't imagine the kind of person I'd be today if I had grown up there. Would I ever have had the confidence to transition?

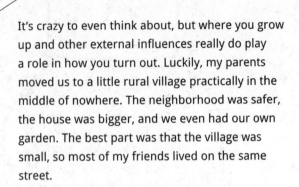

It's crazy to even think about, but where you grow up and other external influences really do play a role in how you turn out. Luckily, my parents moved us to a little rural village practically in the middle of nowhere. The neighborhood was safer, the house was bigger, and we even had our own garden. The best part was that the village was small, so most of my friends lived on the same street.

The closeness of village life meant that I'd always be on my bike with my friends or getting in trouble with them somewhere. I miss the days spent at the local park with my friends, running up and down the skate ramp, faster and faster until we were high enough to pull ourselves up to the top. We'd spend hours on that rickety old thing, talking about who knows what, thinking we were the shit. Sometimes we might find ourselves on the swings eating strawberry licorice, listening to the greatest hits 2006 had to offer while seeing who could jump off the highest.

Nothing particularly interesting ever happened in my little village, so when it did, you remembered it forever.

Like that one time my friend launched off the swing too high and sprained her ankle, or when a crappy

I wouldn't have been caught dead in a dress.

tinfoil barbecue caught fire in the park after being stuffed behind a bench. That was a great day—we ended up in the front seats of a fire engine wearing big yellow helmets. Everything was so easy back then. As kids, nobody cared about who you were or what you wore.

From the moment I had the capacity to make my own decisions, I generally steered clear of anything pink, frilly, or sparkly. This took my grandparents far too long to realize, and I learned all about faking gratitude at Christmas pretty early on! However, picking out clothes was never really a big deal, and as a kid I'd wear stuff from both the boys' and girls' sections. I wouldn't have been caught dead in a dress unless I had to, and I can only remember two occasions when I did: one time at my aunt's wedding when I was seven...and at a school dance.

The dance was to celebrate graduating middle school when I was thirteen. I spent days searching in shops until I found the most boring long black dress I could. (Even thinking about it

makes me cringe.) Trust me, a dress wasn't my first choice—if I could have, I would have thrown on pants and a shirt. It was no secret that I was a massive tomboy, and the thought of everyone gawking at me because I wasn't in my typical sweatpants-and-T-shirt ensemble was terrifying. But my parents were sure that if I did turn up in pants, I would get bullied. I felt so defeated knowing that people would have something to say no matter what I wore. At least by wearing the stupid dress, I'd make my parents happy.

On the night of the dance, I was literally pinned against the bathroom wall by my mum, who was desperately trying to put makeup on my face.

At first I let her do it out of curiosity—I'd never put makeup on before, and maybe I'd like it? NOPE. I didn't even have to look at myself in a mirror to know that it made me feel so wrong. All I could think about was the weight of the makeup on my lips and the dark circles around my eyes. When I did finally look in the mirror, I saw my long hair and its signature part down the middle, but for once instead of a ponytail, it was awkwardly draped over my bony shoulders. In my opinion, most thirteen-year-olds who try to put on makeup look like three-foot-tall middle-aged women, and I was no different. I was a pale, gaunt figure with spiderlike mascara and brown lipstick: hot.

I felt confused and angry. I wasn't angry at my mum
for making me try it, but angry at myself for not
enjoying getting dressed up, like I felt I was supposed
to. Instead, I felt completely repulsed by my reflection,
and I ran downstairs to scrub the mess off my face.
I hopped into my dad's car and was driven to the
"dance." I use the word lightly. In reality it was a dimly
lit hall with a crappy DJ, a handful of jelly beans on each
table, and teachers serving squash, a sugary fruit juice.

Apart from that night, my parents were really
supportive of my fashion choices when I was growing
up, as long as I was happy. They didn't give in without
trying, though. The last time we ever clashed on this
was when I was picking out an outfit for my last day at
school, when I was sixteen. The tradition for anyone
on their last day was to not wear their school uniform
but still dress formally. By this point, I had come to
terms with the fact that I was trans and was beginning
to gain confidence at presenting as more masculine,
so there was no way I was wearing "girls' clothes."

I'm sure my parents didn't expect me to wear a dress,
but I think they were hoping I'd opt for a button-up
blouse and some girls' pants or something. I had
other ideas. Most of my wardrobe comprised of
guys' clothes, but I didn't have anything formal.
When shopping with my family one day, I stopped
in the men's aisle and starting browsing for a shirt
and tie. My dad didn't like that idea, but I stood by

THIS is it.
STOP
trying
TO hide
who ARE.
you

the fact that I wouldn't want anything else and that it didn't matter to anyone but me. We rarely got into arguments, but on that day something just clicked within me that said, *This is it. Stop trying to hide who you are.* Looking back at the pictures of that final school day is so great because you can see how genuinely happy I was. Everyone wants to be able to look back at their last school pictures, so I love that I have some that I don't feel uncomfortable looking at.

Sorry, Dad. The argument was worth it.

It wasn't just clothes; from as young as six, I was referred to as a tomboy by my friends, teachers, and parents. My very best friend was named James, and for years we were inseparable on the playground. People probably thought I had a crush on him, but he was just my best friend. In fact, for most of my childhood I only managed to have one female friend. I don't think that was a purposeful decision, I just got along better with guys because of our similar interests. This had its downsides, though—some hobbies were gender-specific, like football or Scouts. I wanted to be in Scouts so bad; I remember being green with envy at all my friends coming into school after their camping trips with stories and jokes I couldn't understand.

I guess to some people that seems like an obvious early sign that I wasn't happy with my gender, but that's a huge misconception. I don't think I was even aware of a divide between "girl" and "boy" stuff when I was young: my parents thankfully let me pick whatever I wanted and didn't make a big deal out of some things "only being for boys."

I know some trans guys who grew up in environments where female gender roles were really harshly enforced. They'd be stuck with dresses, dolls, makeup, and pink everything. But guess what? They still ended up transitioning to male. These kinds of stories are hard for a lot of trans guys to admit I think, because they don't want their childhoods to invalidate their identities, but they show that

gender identity is so deep in our core that no amount of conditioning will change it.

As much as I'd like my childhood to have been less clichéd, I can't help the fact that I wore "boys' clothes" and played with "boys' toys." I naturally went toward action figures, cars, Lego, and crafty stuff—although if I'm being completely honest, I have to admit that yes, Alex Bertie did have his fair share of Barbie dolls at one point.

The birth of my sister, Hollie, when I was six was a great yet very weird thing for me and everyone else in my family. Weird in the sense that Hollie grew up consistently being a "girly girl." Seeing her so at ease with femininity and her body was hard to watch because we were brought up in the same way. This proves that it wasn't how I was raised that led to me transitioning, but at the time it only added to my gender confusion. It was difficult for my mum too, as she'd never had to deal with anyone borrowing her makeup or clothes before—I was more interested in trying on my dad's vests and shoes! Hollie and I have never really been inseparable like other "sisters" can be, and I'm not sure if that's because of the large age gap between us or because of how different our interests are. I was never there to give her fashion advice or teach her how to use makeup—instead we wrestled and played video games.

Until I was about eleven, I didn't have any concept of gender dysphoria and certainly had no idea what being transgender meant. But I think if I had been exposed to these terms earlier, I definitely would have identified with them. At that early stage I wasn't analyzing my passing thoughts, like

Alex Bertie did have his fair share of Barbie dolls at one point.

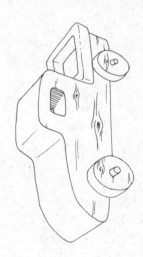

the envy I felt toward my male peers or why my interests were so different from those of other girls. Instead, I was just me. My only real concern in life was what I was going to watch on TV when I got home from school.

When I look back at my younger years, I'm pretty sure I was fairly content.

The pictures from when I was two years old are pretty funny, because in some I look like a little boy. There are pictures of me standing in my crib with short blond hair spiking out in every direction, and similar ones at the beach. Pictures of my childhood where I look more androgynous make me happy— not because I'm ashamed of any previous femininity, but because I feel like those images connect with who I am now. It's easy to look back and feel like I missed out on a "male childhood," but I've come to terms with the fact that it is what it is and at the time, I was happy.

I've seen stories online of kids coming to terms with their trans identities at really young ages, with the support of their parents, and I have mixed emotions about it. On one hand, it's amazing that these kids (A) have support and (B) get to experience more of their lives identifying as their true selves. If I'd realized my identity early on, I could've gone on

At the TIME, I was HAPPY

hormone blockers and stopped female puberty before it started, or felt more confident in school, sparing me from getting bullied relentlessly. But on the other hand, figuring it out sooner wouldn't have made testosterone (T) or surgery happen sooner; those things have age restrictions and I couldn't have started T until I was seventeen years old.

I don't know what I would have preferred.

Discovering myself sooner would have meant I'd have been able to experience having a male childhood, as well as not needing chest surgery, thanks to hormone blockers. However, I still would've had to wait until I was seventeen to get hormones, so I would have spent way longer dealing with the dysphoria.

So maybe finding myself a little later in life was better for me. Although I missed out on some experiences, like my dad teaching me how to shave or going to Scouts, I was able to focus on being a happy, naive kid. Granted, I went through hell when I finally realized and eventually had to have a pretty invasive surgery to get rid of the "blessings" of female puberty…but still. I don't think I could've dealt with that emotional pain as a child.

It's actually pretty awkward talking about my childhood to people I meet now, especially if they don't know I was assigned female at birth. There are certain things I have to leave out or vaguely gloss over, like how I never played rugby in school or that I took swimming classes with girls.

I think that's one of the reasons I find it easier to come out as trans sooner rather than later to people I know I'm going to be spending a lot of time with. The last thing I want is to feel like I have to watch every word I say in case I out myself by accident, or end up lying about certain elements of my past to keep things a secret.

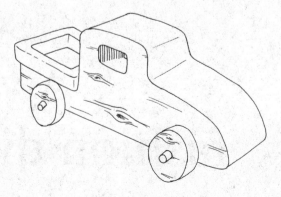

3

BECOMING A TEEN

I was an
introverted,
socially
awkward
fashion disaster.

Like most people, the beginning of my teenage years was absolutely horrible. I was an introverted, socially awkward fashion disaster. Seriously: if I could go back in time to any moment, I'd go back to the time I bought some boxing shoes and set them on fire. They weren't a good look, Baby Alex!

I've only ever been to one school dance, the one when I was leaving middle school at thirteen, and it sucked. You'd think I'd want to remember my one and only school dance, right? Wrong. About two weeks before the big day, I got myself a girlfriend—which at the time was a huge deal because I still identified as female. It was the first time anyone in my school had been exposed to lesbians, so it didn't go down too well. The first person I told spilled my secret to someone else, who told someone else, until eventually the whole school knew. By the next day, kids were crowding around

me and my girlfriend, staring and asking if it was true. I hadn't even told my parents yet. So, not only was I under pressure to wear a dress at the dance and look sickeningly feminine, but most of my friends didn't want to associate themselves with me either.

Being out isn't as glamorous as it's made out to be, especially at thirteen when you're trying so hard to make your parents believe that *No, it's not a phase*, while actually still trying to figure yourself out. When I started high school, the negativity surrounding my sexuality came with me.

Everyone knew that I was The Lesbian from rumors and gossip. I didn't stand a chance.

The biggest fear you have when starting a new school is *What if nobody likes me?* Looking back, I'm sure there were only a small number of people who genuinely didn't like me, but when the fear of people talking about me behind my back was hanging over my head, it was incredibly difficult to open up. Going into my first day of school, my only goal was to make just one friend. But as I looked around the classroom, all I could see was confident people— people you could just tell from the first glance were going to become popular.

IT was
INCREDIBLY
difficult
to
OPEN
up.

The school was big and old and had a really confusing layout, so I spent most of my first few weeks feeling nervous as hell and getting lost all the time. Not too far into the start of my first semester, my girlfriend told me she had a crush on a boy in her class. I think we broke up, but I don't remember the conversation—it was clearly a really mature, adult relationship....

Anyway, losing my girlfriend left me in pieces and at lunch I sat on my own to wallow in self-pity. I didn't have many friends because I'd been stupid enough to only hang out with that one girl, so I was preparing myself to be alone for a long time. That's when four kids with dark swoopy hair came up to me and asked if I was okay. They were a bunch of emo kids and I had no idea why they were talking to me, but I guess I probably looked a lot like them in my sorry state...just not intentionally.

I explained what happened, and I think as soon as they realized that I wasn't straight, they pretty much claimed me as one of their own.

Our group of friends was scattered around different classes for most of the week, but during every break we'd find each other in our spot of choice: the art room. We were a mismatched bunch, with supposed "flaws" making us unfortunate targets for those

The most accepting people at school were the ones who were shat on by their classmates.

blessed with popularity. Together we endured snide comments in the classroom, dodged various projectiles hurled from lunchboxes, and protected each other from the harshness of other students. It's definitely funny how life throws you together with like-minded people. We weren't all the same—in fact, some couldn't have been more different and argued all the time—but sometimes you have to take what you're given. It baffles me to this day that the nicest, most accepting people at school were the ones who were shat on by their classmates, whereas those who belittled others for being slightly out of the ordinary were put on pedestals.

I was so moody as a teenager. It was strange, because I never used to stand up to bullies, but I was aggressive and hotheaded toward other people when something didn't go my way. One time, a friend and I got into an argument and ended up getting in each other's faces (our heads were together, pushing against each other like billy goats) in the middle of school. We were shouting and shoving each other, but despite

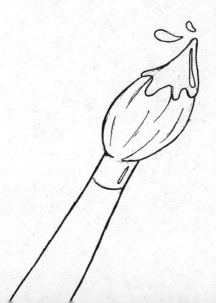

him being waaaay stronger than me, I wouldn't back down. Eventually some guy came over and pulled us apart, which was probably for the best.

I wasn't the smartest of kids in school, but I didn't struggle either. I really liked physics, religious education, and history, but I didn't get great grades. I also studied French for six years, and at first I really hated it. I think this was because it involved so much speaking, and I was too shy to say anything in case I pronounced it wrong. But in my last year of school, I had a new French teacher named Mr. Hook.

I'm not sure if he was gay, but he was really effeminate and everyone used to mess with him.

My being openly LGBTQ+ at this point meant that we were in the same boat, and I think he could tell. Coming into his class made me feel normal and relatively untouchable, so I really looked forward to French every week.

For as long as I can remember, I've always been creative. I chose to study graphic design and art, with the idea that I'd be able to work digitally in one class and more traditionally in the other. Despite not anticipating any high grades, I finished school with an A in art! This might have had something to do with the fact that the art room was the only safe place in the school at lunchtime, but I really did enjoy painting and drawing as well. Unfortunately, graphic design class was awful and I hated it.

I was picked on relentlessly and the projects we were given sucked.

Most of what we did involved putting our heads in a book rather than a mouse in our hands, which infuriated me. I left school with a C and all interest in the subject gone. It wasn't until I started college years later that I rediscovered my love for design.

Outside of school I didn't really go out much; I spent my time doing art, browsing the internet, or playing video games with my friends. I spent hours in front of a screen with a controller in my hand, and in fact I still do. There's something amazing and addictive about all the different stories you step into when playing games, and I genuinely think this has something to do with how creative I am today.

When I was thirteen I started to make YouTube videos and learn how to use editing software. I can't even begin to express how bad they were. At the time, lip-syncing was really popular, so I'd spend hours putting together little music videos with different camera angles and effects. I was amazed by the idea

I couldn't stand the discomfort I felt about being so exposed around other people.

of "green screening," where if you film in front of a green background, you can replace the green with whatever you like. My dad has always been really supportive of my "creative endeavors," so when I asked him to paint one of my bedroom walls bright green, it was done within a week.

The time I spent hiding away in my room from the outside world was where I learned some of the most valuable information I know. Not only did I start a YouTube channel, but I found communities online that taught me so much about the world and the people in it. I learned about different gender identities, sexualities, cultures, sex, and relationships, and even how to communicate with people. There were some people in real life who never even gave me a chance, so the only way I could interact with people outside my group of misfits was the internet. I'd play online games and go into chat rooms to make new friends who couldn't judge me before they knew me. When anyone judges a person based on how much time they spend on the internet, I can't help but laugh. That person on their computer is probably accessing more information and talking to more people than the person trying to put them down. It makes me wonder what these "superior beings" do with their time to make it that much more valuable. I'll never regret the monstrous amount of time I've spent (and still spend) on the internet, because I think I'm more of an accepting person thanks to the people I've met online.

Throughout school I tried to suppress my negative body image feelings, but the breaking point came after having to take swimming class in our PE lessons for three semesters in a row. I actually like swimming a lot and took regular lessons before going to high school, so it wasn't the swimming part that I hated. I couldn't stand the discomfort I felt about being so exposed around other people. Even in the most basic one-piece swimsuit, I felt horrible. It clung to me in every way, not leaving anything to the imagination. I began to get my mum to write notes claiming I had every injury under the sun, just to get out of it. Soon after, I began missing whole days of school to get out of it. Eventually my teachers confronted me and I had no choice but to express how miserable swimming class made me.

They gave me two options:
1. Get changed in the handicapped stalls away from the girls and wear a shirt over the swimsuit. The

shirt was actually a good idea, but I hated the thought of standing out so much and being the one weird kid who wore clothes in the pool. In hindsight, I wish I had started getting changed in the handicapped stalls, because when the self-hate started getting worse, I began putting on all my PE clothes under my school uniform before going to school. That was gross, and in summer the heat was unbearable.

2. Change to a co-ed PE class. This group had both boys and girls, but the PE options were limited to completely noncontact sports and the group was for all the kids who hated exercise. I really liked sports, so it was depressing to attempt PE without anyone else playing the games properly, but anything was better than swimming with the girls.

The time I took off to avoid swimming combined with the time I had to stay home because of bullying meant that my grades were bound to suffer in some way. Luckily the only thing that slipped was history, and I didn't care much about it anyway. Still, hiding away and trying to ignore my problems was the worst thing I could have done. It's a slippery slope because the more time you take off, the harder it is to get back into a routine. You begin to dread going back to school, building it all up in your head to be worse than it actually is.

It wasn't until I started to stop caring about what other people thought of me that the issues began to show signs of improvement.

> In school I was so worried about people judging me for the way I dressed or how I acted that, after trying to change myself for them, I didn't even know what I wanted for myself. The first thing I did after leaving school was buy a bunch of new clothes to reinvent myself the way I wanted to be. I mean, I wasn't exactly fresh off the catwalk, but I was happy!

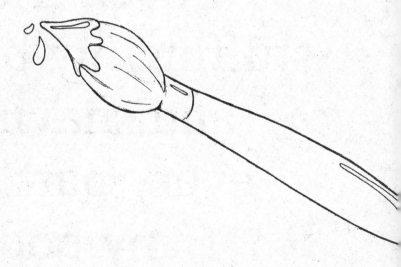

4

PUBERTY & SELF-HATE

I even tried
stuffing my bra
and shaving
every part of
my body.

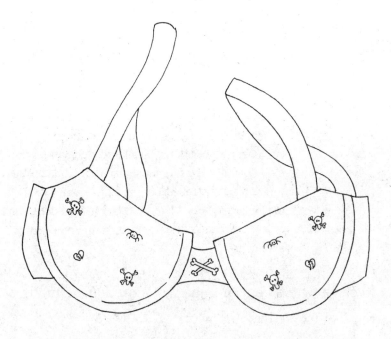

"When did you know you were trans?" is something
I hear all too often. My response is always the same:
it's a long story. I didn't just wake up one day and
realize I was a boy. Instead, it took years of anxiety,
low self-esteem, confusion, sadness, and even a
two-week phase of being as feminine as possible.
However, generally speaking, I realized something
wasn't quite right when I reached puberty. The girls
I knew at school were loving and embracing their
changes, but I only felt jealous of the guys whose
voices were breaking.

I had hoped that puberty might bulk me up a little,
but it never did. I'm naturally really skinny, which
must be down to genetics, because my mum is
exactly the same. My metabolism is fast—great

because I can eat shit without seeing the side effects, but awful because my insides are probably rotting to hell. Before I started hormone treatment when I was twenty, I was skinny in all the wrong places and hated my thin arms. It got so bad that I didn't like wearing short-sleeved T-shirts because they made me look frail. I don't know if this was a gender thing, or just a general self-hate thing, but it wasn't fun either way.

Every new element of puberty I experienced made me feel worse in some way.

Ladies, you think your period is bad? Trust me, being a man and going through that is enough to completely crush any sense of self-confidence you have. When the period first came, I remember being excited because everybody else saw it as this rite of passage into womanhood, but after the first day I was completely over it and wanted it gone. After I started identifying as male, it got so much worse— and not just because of dysphoria.

Using public restrooms as a trans person is scary enough, but "manstruating" and needing to use a public bathroom is even worse. To start, you can't use an aid like a stand-to-pee device (basically a tube to pee through so you don't have to sit or find a cubicle) because it'd be horrific, and there's nowhere

to put your sanitary items once you're done because trash cans in men's restroom are rare. There's also no safe way of combining pads and boxers—it just doesn't work. I'd end up having to double up on underwear just to feel comfortable. If I'd had the money, I would've invested in some special boxers designed for trans men on their period that are really discreet and mean you don't have to wear a pad. But considering I was a broke art student, it didn't take long before it got to the point that as soon as Shark Week started to happen, that was it—I wasn't leaving the house for a week.

Then there was the development of breasts. That word makes me uncomfortable even now, when I have none. My chest was really tiny, which prompted some very confusing feelings for me—I couldn't tell if I hated or loved having a small chest.

All the other girls wanted their chests to grow, but it was obvious I didn't care and it made me stand out.

After a while I started wearing baggy clothes and hunching my shoulders to hide my chest because it made me so uncomfortable.

Going through puberty was the first time I'd ever experienced body image issues, and it took a lot of experimenting to figure out what exactly was causing me all the discomfort. At first I thought I just felt ugly, so I found the most popular girls' hairstyle and got my hair cut. This made everything even worse; I basically got emo bangs cut into my hair, which meant I couldn't tie it back into my signature ponytail. Instead, I had to stick my bangs to my head with hairspray and bobby pins just to get it out of my face. Next, I tried getting all the "cool" clothes. Vans, black skinny jeans, and plaid shirts were all really cool at the time. To my surprise, it made me look better on the outside, but it still didn't change how I felt about myself on the inside. On a whim, I even tried stuffing my bra and shaving every part of my body in the hopes it'd make me feel better about myself. Yep...opposite effect. It didn't take long before I went back to wearing tracksuits and sneakers.

It was so difficult, because I couldn't figure out why I hated my body, especially when everybody else seemed to love what was happening to theirs.

In truth, I was experiencing discomfort because my body didn't match the gender in my head. I wish I could go back in time and give myself the term for that feeling: body dysphoria. But I didn't know the phrase back then, let alone understand it. I didn't

Every time I was at my lowest, I'd hurt myself.

realize it, but I was a boy stuck in a girl's body.

Not being able to "fix it" made me start to lose all hope. The confusion and frustration was so bad that I began to self-harm. I'm not going to get into the details, but it opened up a door to a place from which I couldn't escape for three years. Hurting myself just seemed to ground me in reality when my head felt like it was filled with sorrow. It was the only thing I could find that had any effect, and the release became addictive. Every time I was at my lowest, I'd hurt myself.

I always had to hide the parts of my body that were subjected to it, which was especially hard in summer. Once, I was on the bus coming home from college and a girl with bright hair and an Ed Sheeran shirt was sitting opposite me. I was wearing long sleeves and pants to cover any marks, although in reality I should have been wearing shorts and a T-shirt. That boiling summer day, I couldn't help it—I had to roll my sleeves up. About halfway home, I could feel the girl

watching me, and I saw her eyes go from the top of my forearm, to my eyes, then finally back out the window. Realizing that something was showing, I pulled my sleeves down and shifted uncomfortably in my seat. The girl turned back around and gave me the most sympathetic, understanding look before standing up and walking off the bus. She was trying to be nice, but I just felt so disappointed in myself for letting my guard down.

I wasn't self-harming for attention. If I had been, I'd be able to own up to it by now. Instead, it pulled me back to Earth when my head was spinning out of control with sadness and self-hate, and at the time I didn't realize that there were better ways to deal with my feelings.

My mum isn't stupid and I know she noticed it, but whenever she tried to confront me about it, I'd just lock myself away.

Parents can't check all the boxes, especially if you're upset and need someone who you're certain won't respond negatively or make it worse through punishment. I think if I'd had someone trustworthy to talk to, things would have been a lot easier. You know, someone you can talk seriously to or laugh with. Instead of responding to self-harm with anger, people need to offer support.

ONE day i JUST told MYSELF THAT was enough ENOUGH.

I worked on keeping calm when I got really upset or angry.

The self-harm continued until I was seventeen and in college. I stopped for a number of reasons, the main one being that I began to distract myself when I started getting worked up. I was pretty destructive and hotheaded at the time, and hurting myself was always a very quick decision that I would regret right after—not good. So I worked on keeping calm when I got really upset or angry, which helped me find better coping mechanisms.

Stopping wasn't even a huge revelation. One day I just told myself that enough was enough, and from then on I worked hard not to do it again. It was so difficult to stay away, but I had to remember that there were positive coping mechanisms out there that could help me. For me, two of those were making a video or going on a live-streaming website to be surrounded by people who cared. They would be there to make sure I didn't do something stupid, even if they didn't realize they were being my guardians. Another coping mechanism was to make art, which afterward I'd either rip up or sell. Both outcomes

were equally satisfying! For a while I even wrote in a journal when things got really bad, because by the time I finished writing my feelings down, I felt a lot better. I had to learn along the way never to keep those journals easily accessible though, because they could be pretty triggering.

For those of you who don't know, a trigger is something that sets off a negative reaction.

People have all sorts of triggers—they're not always emotional.

There are also lots of different reactions to triggers—my main one is dysphoria, or general self-hate. There are a number of things that trigger my dysphoria, such as hearing my birth name, being misgendered, or seeing a part of my body that in my mind looks feminine. My latest physical trigger has been my love handles. Just looking at them or feeling someone else touching them really gets to me. (That's why all my shirtless selfies have my body twisted toward the camera—it's all about the angles!) Other triggers can be as small as my hair being slightly too long or as odd as my clothes not fitting right on a given day.

Even after I stopped self-harming, the dysphoria was hard to deal with. Sometimes I'd feel numb, hardly speaking. It's at times like those that I could have

i'd cry
ANGRY,
UGLY
tears.

turned to alcohol, but luckily I didn't feel drawn to drink until I was twenty, way after my worst years. So instead, I found safer means to drown the dysphoria out, locking myself away in my room and trying to escape the negative feelings with video games or internet videos. Then there were the other times, when I couldn't avoid the pain. I'd cry angry, ugly tears. My mind would cloud over and spin with sadness and rage. I'd go on walks in the hopes that the fresh air and buzz of the outside world would snap me out of it. Sometimes it did.

Dealing with it got easier as I began to better understand what would set me off. If I felt myself getting sad, I'd find a distraction. That's the best advice I can give to those struggling with dysphoria: do all that you can to move forward with your transition and keep yourself busy until you're getting what you need.

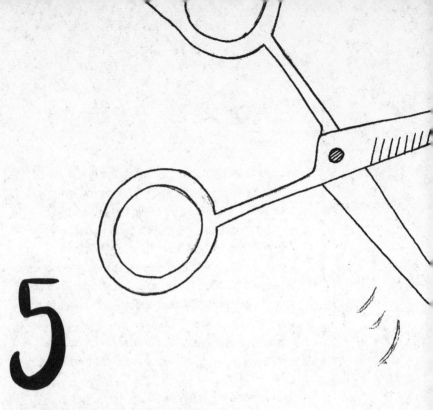

5

THE BIG CHOP

My short hair
was a little
window into a
male identity.

All you need to say to a trans guy is "the haircut" and they'll know exactly what you mean. Short hair is often seen by society as more masculine, so the first "male" haircut means a lot for some guys—it can really help cut down the likelihood of being misgendered. It's the big chop.

For fourteen years I had long straight ash blonde hair down to my butt. My mum loved it and it even made some people a little jealous, but fuck, I hated it. I tried doing all sorts of things to it, but every time it'd end up in the same sad old ponytail. Looking back, my hair was probably the first thing that triggered my dysphoria—every time I looked in the mirror it made me hate myself. I honestly thought I looked ugly.

During half-term break in tenth grade, I confessed to my dad how my long hair made me feel, armed with images (evidence) of girls with short hair. It was quite emotional—I think I ended up sobbing in my

bedroom with pictures of Halle Berry up on Google. What a sight. The feelings were complex. At the front of my mind was guilt; considering I already wore "guys' clothes," I knew I was going to look incredibly masculine after the haircut, and I felt bad that I was incapable of being a "normal" child for my parents. Then there was worry about reactions from other people: no one ever understood why I didn't love my long hair. I'd tried to ignore the length, I'd even tried getting it styled into a "girl cut." But whatever I tried, I still hated it. There was only one other choice: cut it all off.

Getting all your hair cut off is kind of a big deal because yeah, it grows back, but if it looks like crap, you have to deal with it until it does.

With that in mind, I ended up finding a hairstyle previewer online where you could upload an image of yourself and it would impose a different hairstyle on top. God, I wish I had known how to use Photoshop back then. As you can probably imagine, the previewer result was not accurate or perfect, but it helped me to take the leap.

My parents were actually great about it, and by the next week I had an appointment with a local hairdresser. I don't even think I'd picked a style; it was a case of getting there, sitting on a black leather

It was a sort of . . . shaggy mop thing?

sofa, and going through a magazine with my dad until we found one. Eventually I sat in the chair and looked in the mirror while my hair was separated into small ponytails, which were then chopped off one by one. The hairdresser spun me back around and the rest of the staff watched as long locks fell to the floor. I don't remember much of the big reveal other than moving my head and being amazed at how light it felt, then walking outside and not feeling terrible when the wind blew through my hair.

It was a sort of . . . shaggy mop thing? Regardless of how stylish it was, I think you could tell at the time how much of a difference it made to my self-confidence. It was almost like taking a mask off to reveal what had been underneath the whole time. You could finally see *me*.

The reaction from people was kind of amazing. For the first few days, even my mum would say she barely recognized me. Going back to school was definitely interesting. I sat in

class and watched as students entered the room, each one doing a double take and some even flashing huge smiles before saying how great it looked. Obviously it didn't go 100 percent great, and guys who sat behind me snickered and made shallow remarks. But it was liberating; that was the point I realized I'd never win with some people. They'd make fun of me no matter what, so what was the point in letting them ruin my day? I felt so good about the way my short style made me look that I haven't felt bad about my hair since, even though I've been through some pretty bad dye jobs. I'm very, very ginger in my "1 MONTH ON T!" video!

It was actually that group of pea-brained guys who first made a connection between me and being transgender. One day in class they started calling me "Jason," and being confused and annoyed, I listened in on their conversation.

They began talking about the transgender character in a show called *Hollyoaks*, saying I looked like him.

I'd never seen the show, and despite wishing I was male, I had very little knowledge about what being trans actually meant. After school, a Google search told me all I needed to know about Jason. Videos of this transgender guy cutting his hair off and

flattening his chest with bandages popped up.
I still remember the panic I felt sitting in front
of my computer, as if they had found me out.

Still, chopping off all my hair definitely marked the beginning of a serious confidence boost.

I must have had a very masculine-looking face,
because after that haircut strangers called me a
guy about 70 percent of the time, and I wasn't even
trying to present as more masculine. My short hair
was a little window into a male identity and every
time I looked through, I liked what I saw.

Other trans guys ask me how to approach their first
"male" haircut all the time. Actually talking to the
hairdresser can be daunting, I get it. There should
really be a "life skills" class in school that teaches you
stuff like this. My pro tip is to simply find a picture
online of the kind of thing you want and bring it
with you. An actual visualization will definitely get
you both on the same page, whereas "a little off the
top" to you could be a head shave to them. A lot of
people get to know how they like having their hair
by what length it usually gets cut to—it's kind of
like knowing your shoe size. Getting your hair cut is
almost like ordering a fancy coffee. You can be as
vague or as precise as you like, so long as you know
what to say. So what is it that you want? A fade?

Getting your HAIR CUT is ALMOST like ordering A fancy COFFEE.

Squared sideburns? An undercut? The best thing to do is to get online and do some research!

When you look at pictures of me over the last six years, my hair just seems to get shorter and shorter as I've built up confidence over time.

Hair color also has a big impact on my dysphoria, because every time I dye my hair darker, or with a more red tone, I can't even look at myself. So be careful if you think the same might apply to you.

Learning to cut my own hair was one of the best decisions I have ever made. I used to get pretty insecure about my hair growing out too much, because I thought the sides getting too long made my face rounder and more feminine. The problem was that I didn't have the time, confidence, or money to get it cut every couple of weeks to keep it neat, so I'd just get it cut super-short and let it grow. That meant I could never get a "high maintenance" style that looked really clean, and my hair was never the right length all over. So one day when I was completely fed up, I went to Argos and bought some Wahl hair clippers. They were a really basic model and didn't cost a lot, so I knew that even if I couldn't bring myself to try it, I wouldn't have wasted much money.

When I got home, I started looking at videos of people cutting their own hair, which was completely useless. None of them had much of an art to what they were doing, and I could already see that they had developed their own technique that best suited their environment and the hair itself. Not wanting to give up, I started looking at barbering tutorials so I could understand how to properly use the clippers. You're supposed to gradually taper the hair from short at the bottom to longer on top, at the sides, and the back of the head. This was one of my biggest concerns—I didn't want my hair to look choppy, with big lines where it wasn't faded correctly. After doing some research, I began to drag all the mirrors I could find into the bathroom.

I sat on the cold floor with nothing on but boxers because things were about to get pretty hairy. Literally. I put a full-length mirror facing my front, then awkwardly balanced a smaller mirror in the bathtub behind me so I could see the back of my head. Nervously, I parted my hair on both sides of my head to mark where I wanted it to be short and found my grade two clipper guard.

It took a lot of guts to eventually think *fuck it* and just go for it, but it was actually a lot easier to do than I thought.

I shaved all around the sides and back of my head with a two, then moved down to a one to make things even shorter. I dug out the 1.5 guard I had bought online and began to use this to fade out the grade one to the grade two. Next, I spiked my hair up in all directions and used scissors to cut the top, making it longer to the front of my head and shorter at the back by my crown. I think the first time I did it I was in there for almost two hours. My main advice for anyone thinking about cutting their own hair is to learn how to use the tools to create the effect you want, and GO SLOW! When people rush, things go wrong.

Let me give you a little example. It was the day before I was going in for top surgery and I had left cutting my hair to the very last second as I knew I wasn't going to be able to do it myself for a while. I didn't give myself enough time, I was super-nervous, I was using new clippers and wasn't concentrating—so guess what happened? I had my first home haircut "oopsy." I got to the stage

I sat on the cold floor with nothing on but boxers because things were about to get pretty hairy.

where I needed to use the 1.5 guard to blend the sides, so I plopped the guard on the end of the clippers and started messily dragging the clippers over the line. Usually, this part doesn't require much precision, but I really, really wish I had double-checked the guard I put on.

By the time I got halfway around my head, I said out loud to myself, "Wow, this is shorter than I remember!"

Still in a hurry, I glanced quickly at the number on my clippers to check it was a 1.5 and continued a little further. Second-guessing myself one more time, I looked back at the number on the guard, this time actually reading it. It wasn't a 1.5, but a 0.5. I had just shaved the sides of my head practically bald. Luckily I managed to salvage it, but it didn't look great and it was all because I was rushing.

These days I think I do a pretty good job on my hair, and although it takes a little bit longer than if I were to get it done professionally, it's free and really convenient! I cut my hair every one to two weeks to keep it at the perfect length, and I'd definitely recommend that everyone tries it at least once. My hair is a huge part of my self-love, so if you're feeling down, try going in for a fresh cut!

if YOU'RE feeling DOWN, try going in for A FRESH cut.

6

DEALING WITH BULLIES

I was an
easy target.

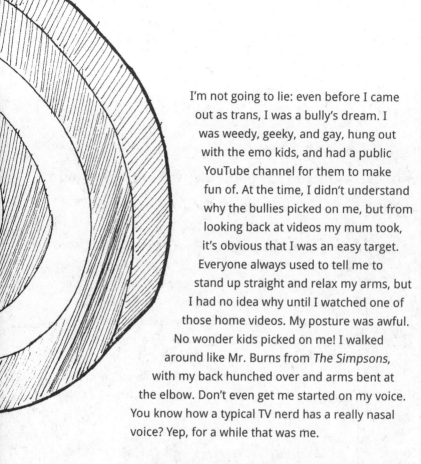

I'm not going to lie: even before I came
out as trans, I was a bully's dream. I
was weedy, geeky, and gay, hung out
with the emo kids, and had a public
YouTube channel for them to make
fun of. At the time, I didn't understand
why the bullies picked on me, but from
looking back at videos my mum took,
it's obvious that I was an easy target.
Everyone always used to tell me to
stand up straight and relax my arms, but
I had no idea why until I watched one of
those home videos. My posture was awful.
No wonder kids picked on me! I walked
around like Mr. Burns from *The Simpsons*,
with my back hunched over and arms bent at
the elbow. Don't even get me started on my voice.
You know how a typical TV nerd has a really nasal
voice? Yep, for a while that was me.

You already know I was unfortunate enough to have
a group of guys in my class who were relentless, but
that was just the beginning. History and graphics
were my top two least favorite classes because
of the people I was grouped with. The worst part
was that these groups stayed the same for three
years. History shouldn't have been that bad, but my
teacher was in charge of dealing with the worst kids
in the school, so she'd dump them in our class when

they were messing up. Bad news for me—it was certain that whoever walked through the door would be someone who disliked me.

There was one particular guy in school that I hated with every fiber in my body. He was one of the most popular guys in our grade and a complete jerk.

He would take the bus home with me, and if I was alone, he would sit next to me, with his two friends in front, boxing me in. On one trip home, he kept pulling out my headphones to ask me offensive questions that no fourteen-year-old should be pressured to answer. He asked me about my nonexistent sex life just because I was bisexual. When I stared out the window in an attempt to ignore him, he began playing music from his phone while bashing it against my head.

My history teacher really liked that guy for some reason, so he ended up spending a lot of time in our class. One time, we couldn't have been in the room for more than ten minutes when he started to tease me about my YouTube channel. I was proud of my channel, but so terrified of that guy that I just burst into tears. I was so scared of what was to come that I couldn't even help myself. The teacher pulled me out of class and asked what was wrong.

When I told her, she demanded that I delete my YouTube channel. How screwed up is that? Instead of disciplining the bully, she punished the victim.

She wasn't the only unhelpful teacher. Every single one thought they had their own way of fixing the problem. One told me to simply ignore them. Reality check: I was already trying to ignore them because I was too terrified to do anything else! Another told me to stand up for myself. Hello? The police don't tell little old ladies to stand up for themselves when some brute is trying to steal their purse! One teacher actually decided it was the bully who needed help and rewarded him on the rare occasions that he wasn't being a dick. It's one thing to try to help someone if they're struggling with academics; it's another thing entirely to sympathize with them if they're harassing someone else.

Who knows why bullies do what they do? Frankly, it doesn't matter. Bullies need to be made to face the consequences of their actions.

Being victimized is serious, because mistreatment sticks with you years after you leave the bullies behind. Even now, when I hear rowdy thirteen-year-olds having seemingly harmless "banter," it takes me straight back to the classroom.

I don't know why that day was different, but something snapped within me.

A tutor is supposed to be the first port of call in a situation like this, but mine was awful and no help at all. You know how some people are just oblivious to the world around them? People who put their bag next to them on the bus so then old people can't sit down? Yeah, those people. My tutor's attitude was that I should live my life around the bullies, avoiding or ignoring them. His idea of discipline was a "firm talking to," which in reality would make you fall asleep. It's not enough to just tell your students to speak out if they're being bullied, because for a lot them that just won't be an option. It's up to teachers to be perceptive, to see when a bad situation is occurring, and to know how to deal with it so it doesn't happen again.

With no teacher support, I slowly realized that sometimes you have to take things into your own hands. I started sticking up for myself. To be honest, it didn't make the bullies stop, but at least I felt a little better. One time in science class when I was fifteen, some douchebags took it upon themselves to throw things at me and

my friends. I don't know why that day was different, but something snapped within me. After being hit on the back of the head by yet another ball of paper,

I turned in my chair, looked one of them in the eye, and told him to "FUCK OFF."

Obviously they all laughed in my face, so I stood up as calmly as possible and asked them, "What's the point? Don't you have anything better to do than be assholes?" The science teacher was a pushover, so when she failed to do anything, I walked out of the classroom and into the office of my Head of Year.

She was also my gym teacher, so she already knew and liked me. I kind of exploded, explaining everything I had been putting up with from these guys over the last three years. I took the opportunity to explain the issues I had with my gender identity too, and to my surprise she was the first teacher to do something helpful. To start with, she informed my other teachers about what was going on so they'd look out for me more in class. This kind of helped; I was moved closer to the teacher's desk in most cases, but some teachers really drilled into the bullies if they even looked at me the wrong way.

Next, my Head of Year set up a meeting with two of the main pupils at fault to talk to my parents.

i STARTED
sticking
UP for
MYSELF.

While they didn't yet know I was questioning my gender, my parents did know I wasn't straight, so they weren't surprised to learn I was being picked on for being different.

I'd never seen the two boys look so terrified as they did after my dad spoke to them, and I think for a second they might have finally felt guilty after seeing how serious it had all become.

You know what sucks though? I wanted to explain to my parents what had happened before my Head of Year called to arrange the meeting, and I still remember coming home with my tail between my legs. The fact that I felt bad for sticking up for myself is pretty messed up. I told my dad what the guys had been doing, which was rare because I always tried to keep what I had to deal with to myself, so nobody would worry. My dad asked, "Well, what did you do about it?" I quickly responded, "I told them to eff off." The look on his face was shocked to say the least....I don't think he'd ever heard me swear before.

Word travels fast in a huge school, and before long I had people I barely knew patting me on the back and congratulating me for justice being served. The final thing my Head of Year did was to introduce me to a student counselor.

Let this be the proof that sometimes you have to deal with things head on. That doesn't mean being stupid—I never threw anything back, shouted, or added fuel to the fire because that would have only made things worse. I know you've probably heard this one hundred times before, but it's true: bullies do it for a reaction. So instead of giving them the satisfaction of getting upset or angry, you should tell somebody and let them deal with it. If the bullying occurs more than once, keep a log of every instance as evidence and be sure to report each one to a teacher. I made the mistake of keeping things to myself for years, which backfired because when I finally had the courage to tell a teacher, they could only act on the most recent event.

After I finished school at the end of tenth grade, the amount of messages I got on Facebook from people in my classes was ridiculous.

They'd tell me how "brave" I was for being myself, or that they wished we'd spoken more. Those messages made me so mad that I couldn't respond, in case I said something along the lines of *Then why the hell didn't you stand up for me?*

Some of them might have genuinely meant it, but at the time I just saw it as so cowardly. These were people who had sat back and smiled while their friends were cruel.

It's so important to step in or at least report it if you see someone getting bullied. The chances are that the victim is too scared to do anything about it. Besides, you have no idea what someone is going through outside of school, so they might really need support. If the bully is one of your friends, for the love of God, please say something! Your friend is abusing someone, be it verbally or physically, and you're doing nothing to stop it. Stonewall (a UK-based LGBTQ+ rights charity) carried out a campaign a few years ago called "No Bystanders," which was about this exact topic. By watching someone being bullied and doing nothing about it, you're being a bystander. If just one person had stuck up for me in school, I would have instantly felt safer—and my mentality that the whole school hated me could have been fractured.

The chances are that the victim is too scared to do anything about it.

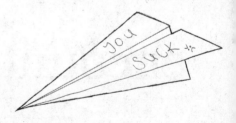

7

GETTING HELP

My first
encounter with a
professional
who validated
how I felt.

At the age of fifteen, I had no idea who to turn to for advice on my gender, so my Head of Year was the first person I told. She directed me toward a student counselor who was based in this tiny shack by the school parking lot. I was a little uneasy about going, because I wasn't ready to have my parents know about my feelings, but she told me that everything would be confidential unless I posed a risk to myself or others. This is the rule that all therapists and counselors follow within the US and UK. Something else that worried me was the fact that this place didn't exactly have a great reputation. It was known around school as the place people went to if they were depressed or pregnant. The first time I walked in, there was a group of sixteen-year-olds who used to sneak off at lunch to smoke, and a bunch of pregnant girls—I couldn't see anyone who was struggling with the same things as me.

My counselor was a lady named Helen. She was really nice, but all I seem to remember about her was these wide eyes. Our sessions were kind of like therapy; I'd see her once a week and we'd just sit and talk about school life, my reactions to problems, and sometimes family stuff. She also encouraged me to get help to reduce the bullying. Helen didn't know much about trans stuff, but she set up a meeting with a local LGBTQ+ organization called Over the Rainbow that supported young people.

That was my first encounter with a professional who validated how I felt, gave me a word to describe my pain, and told me what kind of treatment I could look for in the future.

They were youth workers who explained that I was expressing feelings related to being transgender and that the pain I had when looking at certain parts of myself was called body dysphoria.

They gave me an information packet with loads of trans terms. I specifically remember the term "packing" with a clip art image of a lunchbox, which I now know means to put something in your underwear to give the appearance of a bulge. The youth workers avoided directly explaining this one to me because I was just taking my first baby steps into the topic and probably didn't want to jump straight into talking about my genitals.

So packing was in the information packet, but there was no mention of binding either there or from the youth workers themselves, which was kind of odd. Binding is the act of compressing your chest to make it flatter, but the closest the youth workers got to talking about this was noticing how hunched over my body language was and explaining that it might be a

There are so many trans personalities in the spotlight.

reaction to a part of my body that I didn't like.

At the back of the packet was a list of trans celebrities, which was really unhelpful because I couldn't identify with any of them. Half of them were drag queens and it even included FTM porn star Buck Angel. While all of them were breaking down barriers in their own way, there was nobody in there that I could relate to. Thankfully, education and resources have improved drastically in the six years since then. There are so many well-known trans personalities in the spotlight thanks to the increased diversity in TV, film, and especially on YouTube. Most of the young people I meet have trans YouTubers like Chase Ross or Stef Sanjati to look up to. These are people who put out appropriate, educational content for kids of a similar age to themselves. It's fantastic.

Being given the term "transgender" to describe what I felt was

THiS was medical; it REQUIRED a diagnosis.

simultaneously the best and worst thing to ever happen to me. Best in that I finally knew I wasn't broken or ill, but worst in that at fifteen I had no idea where to go from there. Like, yeah, I'm different, but what now? It's not like discovering your sexuality, where it's more of a personal, emotional thing. This was medical; it required a diagnosis. I didn't know anything about that when I was fifteen.

That being said, the word "transgender" opened a door that led me to find support online through videos and blogs.

I discovered whole communities of people who made me feel like I wasn't so different and alone. Initially I found an American trans YouTuber in his twenties named Skylar who had been on testosterone for years and was going through surgery at the time. He'd also uploaded these transition timelines where he'd compare his body and voice every month to years gone by, to show his changes. Sky's videos were a whole new world for me; I had no idea someone as young as he was could transition, or how much hormone treatment and surgery could do to help ease dysphoria. That was the first time I ever felt jealous of another person's transition though, and it prevented me from getting too invested in his videos. It probably also didn't help that he was in America, which meant that the health care system was completely different. Still, he gave me hope that I might be able to transition one day in the future.

I also found a lovely Scottish lady named Linzi who made a lot of videos on sexuality. Linzi's videos really helped me understand that sexuality can be fluid, and that you can like who you like without having to always label it. She had 3,000 subscribers, and I looked up to her so much for her intelligence and her ability to gain a substantial supportive following while vlogging about a subject I had always been bullied about. She later played a big part in inspiring my own video-making—one of my first really successful videos was my coming-out story in response to her.

Today, those online communities and resources are 1,000 times stronger than they were then, and it's just a few years later.

It makes me really proud to think that my generation has built something that will help kids like myself. Thanks to websites like Tumblr and YouTube, it's possible for anyone to broadcast their story and attract huge communities.

Looking back, I'm not sure why I was so resistant to asking for help in the "real world." Was I scared that someone would tell my parents? Maybe I thought I'd get picked on even more? I don't know, but getting help was the best thing I could have done for myself. Suddenly my teachers looked out for me in class, I wasn't forced to get changed with girls or attend swimming classes anymore, and by the end of the school year I could face a bully and tell them to stop. It didn't fix all of my problems, but it definitely made school more bearable. And when I opened up to one person, it started a chain reaction that led to me sharing my transition with hundreds of thousands of people today.

Asking for help is difficult, especially if you don't realize you need it.

But if you're questioning your gender, you need to reach out. There's no harm in going to see someone to explain your feelings, so long as you make sure they're qualified. If you don't get an answer from them that you're satisfied with, you can always go and see someone else for a second opinion. I've had to deal with many so-called professionals who have ended up being wrong, so it's important to go with your gut. Bear in mind that many doctors or mental health professionals don't know that much about trans issues, so do your research and ask for someone with experience if you can.

8

CHEST BINDING

The job of a
binder is to
compress you.

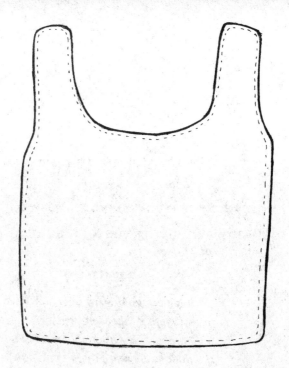

I'll always remember my last day of school. Not only was it the first day that filled me with confidence and hope, but it was also the day I finally got my first real chest binder.

I never had a very large chest and it was barely visible under clothes, but it was a huge part of my discomfort and body dysphoria. Months before the end of school, I had fallen into a pit of self-hatred. At the time I had no idea how to move forward or how to tell my parents I was trans. So I turned to my YouTube channel as a form of release. I posted a video of me crying in front of a camera with the slightly dramatic title "Transgender Suffering," which attracted a whopping 1,000 views at the time. Many viewers offered words of advice and support to me, which meant a lot.

While that video was difficult to make, it did result in something that changed my life.

I opened my email soon after I posted it to find a total stranger offering me a brand-new binder for free.

In hindsight, this person could have been anyone, and yet I still broke the golden rule of the internet: never give out your address. At first it took them a while to convince me, because I was really reluctant to accept something for nothing, especially when the something carried a pretty hefty price tag. But I was only sixteen, I had no access to money or any way of ordering something from the internet, and I wasn't ready to come out to my parents yet. With that in mind, I handed over my address to the generous stranger. I still remember the feeling of relief as I squeezed myself into my new binder when I got home from my last day of school.

Anything that compresses your chest is a binder, so they come in all different shapes and sizes. Some look like vests and fasten together with Velcro, clasps, or zips. Others are strapless and just look like a sheet that wraps around your chest. Binders can be made from various materials including polyester mesh and cotton; each material has its pros and cons, so do your research to find one that's right for you.

My chest made me feel terrible just by looking down.

Some people wear tight sports bras and others even make their own DIY binders. For some trans men, their chest can play a big part in their dysphoria, as breasts are seen as a female trait. For me personally, I found that going out in public without binding my chest made it more likely that I would be misgendered, and my chest made me feel terrible just by looking down. Having something permanently attached to you that you feel isn't supposed to be there can be pretty distressing.

You could argue that my very first binder, before the generous gift from the stranger, was one I DIYed myself with a little help from my mum. I took a one-piece swimsuit that was slightly too small, cut the bottom off it, rolled it up into a sports-bra shape, and asked my mum to hem it. It rode up under my clothes, but I still wore it to school a few times to see if it made me feel any better about my chest, and it did! It was a huge step that helped me realize that my chest

made me uncomfortable, and it became the gateway
into my discovery of all things trans.

The job of a binder is to compress you, which does
leave you aching after a while. There is no nicer
feeling than coming home and taking a binder off.
The tightness does pose more of a problem in the
summer months; the materials aren't very breathable
so they make you melt in the heat. It goes the other
way too: in the chilly seasons, I'd absolutely dread
getting out of my toasty warm bed to put on an ice-
cold binder. Oh, and don't even get me started on
trying to pull one of those things on after a bath has
left you damp.

A bath is as far as I got for a long time—for five years,
I never went swimming.

I didn't want to be the only guy fully clothed at the
pool, and the possibility of getting sand in my binder
from swimming in the sea was just too uncomfortable
to think about.

You can get special swimming binders now, but
they're SO expensive! I definitely didn't have the cash
for that. Binders were pricey when I first started out,
which was difficult as a broke art student. As a result,
I wore the same binder every day. If I needed to
clean it, I just had to deal with my chest for however

long it took to dry. Binding also restricted my fashion choices. I couldn't wear anything white or with a wide neckline because the binder would be seen. It was like having to wear a black vest underneath my clothes at all times. I stopped being able to remember what my clothes felt like against my skin, so the first thing I did after surgery was put on ALL my clothes to feel each different material.

I wish I had some way of repaying the stranger who was so generous to me all those years ago, but I have never been able to track down the emails they sent me.

As an alternative way of "giving back," I arranged a fundraiser a couple of years ago with a binder charity in the UK. It donates new binders and repairs old ones to give to young people in positions like mine. In only a few days, we managed to raise £1,000 (about $1,300 in the United States), and the increased awareness inspired many people to donate their old binders, stocking the charity's catalog for months. Once again, I was shocked by how selfless the donors were in helping out vulnerable strangers.

I bound my chest for five years and it never caused any serious side effects. There's a common misconception that binding will damage your health,

and a lot of parents hold it over their trans kids in either genuine worry or as something to deter them from transitioning. But here's the truth: it's only going to actually hurt you if you're doing it wrong.

My general guide to binding is:

Always wear the correct size binder.
Most websites will have a measuring guide, so look at it carefully. Don't be afraid to return a binder if it's too big or too small. A smaller binder won't automatically flatten you more—it's more likely to just hurt you. However, if you're *truly* between measurements, I'd buy the smaller one; most binders will break in and adjust to your body shape after a short time.

Don't bind for extended periods of time.
The recommended maximum binding time is eight-to-ten hours per day, which can be difficult if you have to go to school or work, but trust me. You don't want to wear a binder for too long because it'll leave you with aches and all sorts of other complications. This is especially true for new binders. Take your time when breaking it in, because the more you do, the longer you'll be able to wear it in one go. After a couple of months of breaking a binder in to allow it to shape to my body, I found I could go a whole day before getting uncomfortable at all.

Do not bind while you sleep.
As awkward as your chest makes you feel, you don't want to be restricting your breathing or your blood circulation while you sleep. If you find yourself in a position where you absolutely need to wear your binder—for example, if you're sharing a room with people who don't know you're trans—you might want to think about layering up T-shirts to pad yourself out. If you absolutely have to wear something, use something with minimal compression.

Over the course of my time binding, I tried out a few different styles and brands. I can reassure you that just because a binder is cheap, that doesn't mean it will do a bad job. You can get binders from China on eBay for a few dollars that actually work pretty well. They're made out of a really thin, cheap material but they don't look half bad and have a good amount of compression. Having said that, I wouldn't recommend them for someone with a larger chest. The larger your chest, the more strain you're going to be putting on the material—so a binder may not last as long if it isn't good quality. Still, one of those cheap binders would be great for somebody on a budget or for when you go swimming. Just make sure you're really careful about the sizing, because a lot of the cheap binders are made overseas where the size guides vary.

I also tried two different binders from a company called Peecock Products, which makes female-to-male

(FTM) aids such as stand-to-pee devices. They sent them to me for free so I could review them, but that wouldn't change my opinion of them. One fastens with Velcro, whereas the other fastens with clasps. Personally, I wish the two types were combined because they both have major flaws. The Velcro one was really easy and quick to get on and off, but the scratchy side of the Velcro stuck out and irritated my skin. The material was also super-thin, so the compression was really uneven—I'd imagine the binder would stretch out after frequent use. The clasped binder used thicker material, which was way better because it was so much sturdier. Unfortunately there were about ten clasps within a really small space, so they were incredibly difficult to do up and undo.

My favorite binder company is Underworks. It doesn't make products specifically for trans people, but it's huge in the FTM community because of its compression vests. They're on the pricey side, but all four binders I bought from Underworks lasted really long—they never degraded to the point where they were unusable. The binders just looked like cotton vests from the outside, with a mesh material on the inside. You can get them with different lengths of compression, but I preferred the ones that only had the mesh over my chest, rather than the whole way down my torso. That was the binder I wore all the time and it worked so well for my body shape that I

never wanted to switch. I did try out their "tri-top," which is basically just mesh material with no cotton over the top, but it was really tight.

Not everybody chooses to bind their chests, but those on both sides deserve respect. Before telling someone that they're going to damage their body by binding, it's important to do your research.

Try to support them—there's a good chance that binding will help reduce their dysphoria.

And if a trans man decides he doesn't want to bind, that's okay too. Not all trans people feel the same way about their bodies and some find other means of dealing with dysphoria. For example, sometimes guys will work out a lot to build up their chest muscles and get a more masculine shape.

Even though they can be a hassle, without binders I would never have had the confidence to wear certain clothes, get close to people, or even go outside. I would never have been able to finish my education, find work, or participate in the amazing opportunities I've been given. By helping me cope with my dysphoria, binding helped save my life. I'll always be eternally grateful for it—so if you're a concerned parent reading this, please remember what a difference binding could make to the trans child in your life.

9

COMING OUT TO MY FAMILY

It can be terrifying, but once it's done, it's done.

For a lot of people, coming out is something they do once. It can be terrifying, but once it's done, it's done. For me, it wasn't like that—not only did I come out as "not straight," but I also came out as transgender...an equally and perhaps even scarier admission.

For a long time, I didn't feel like I could open up about my feelings to my dad. Sexuality and dating just weren't the kinds of thing we spoke about—we talked about video games, not feelings. As a result, my mum had to deal with a lot of my problems on her own. All teenagers give their parents grief (I have my own teenage sister as proof. Sorry, Hollie!), but not all teenagers are pansexual and transgender. I feel bad every day for what my mum had to go through in the beginning.

At thirteen, I told her that I wasn't straight. I couldn't tell her if I was completely gay, bi, or something else, which must have been really difficult and confusing for her. In addition to the bombshell, I also had to tell her that it was already public knowledge thanks to being outed at school—and that the girl who was my "best friend," who always stayed over, was in fact my girlfriend. As you can imagine, it didn't go well. At the time, I resented my mum for responding negatively. I misunderstood her frustration as her not accepting my sexuality at all, when in reality she was more upset that the whole school knew before she did. From her point of view, the damage had already been done and there was nothing she could do to protect me. As a result, I tried to hide a lot of the bullying that I went through. This was partly to shield her because I understood how it made her feel, but it was mainly to protect myself—I didn't want to hear her say "I told you so."

My dad found out that I was dating a girl when my mum and my extremely drunk neighbor were yelling at each other in the street. We've never been blessed with good neighbors, but these guys were particularly bad. It must have been nearing midnight and they had their music up way too loud, banging around and having no respect for anyone on a Wednesday night. My mum (a little drunk) went over and started banging on their door while my dad stood watching from afar. Before long, things had escalated.

I was trying to pull my mum away from this witch of a woman when she shouted some abuse and added, "And your lesbian daughter!" at the top of her lungs.

I froze and started to freak out. When I looked over at my house, my dad was gone. The next morning, he came into my room and I started bawling my eyes

I didn't want to hear her say "I told you so."

out. Incredibly, he told me there was nothing wrong with me and he wasn't disappointed. Still, what I learned from both these experiences is to come out to the most important people in your life first if you can.

With that in mind, I came out as transgender to my mum just after I turned sixteen. Unlike when I was outed as a lesbian at school, the situation was completely under my control and I was more focused on my feelings. I wrote her a letter explaining how I felt about my body in great detail—I didn't want to waste my chance to make her understand. At the time we were struggling to communicate about the simplest of things, like what was for dinner or the state of my bedroom, without interruptions or misunderstanding, so writing was the easier option. I remember running a bath before I gave the letter to her, so I had an excuse for the conversation to end if her reaction was negative. I sat next to her while she read it. Her reaction shocked me, because she said that to some extent she already knew. I had always presented as pretty

masculine and my interests sided there too, so it was eye-opening to have my mum agree with me and validate my feelings. It meant more to me than when my school counselor or a youth worker had identified me as trans, because my relationship with my mum wasn't perfect.

Her initial reaction was a mixture of relief and concern. I think she felt grateful that I had opened up to her for once, so she could finally get a better understanding of why I was upset and defensive all the time. On the flipside, as great as being kept in the loop was, it opened up a whole new world of worries for her. From what I could tell, she was mainly worried about my health if I were to want to start hormones or have surgery. It was natural for her to jump to this, even though I was only just starting to go by my chosen name.

My main goal in coming out to my mum was to just tell her. I wasn't expecting any changes, I just wanted her to know.

We ended the conversation with her saying she'd always be there for me no matter what, and that reaction from her was the first step toward repairing our fractured teen-parent relationship. I still knew we had a long way to go and that it wouldn't always end well, but in that moment, iT opened up a whole NEW world OF WORRIES.

it was enough. It's so important to embrace the small victories in the coming-out process.

Despite her positive reaction, I still didn't really feel like I could talk to her about my transition and my feelings about it.

I spent a lot of time feeling sad or angry about my body, and my mum usually got the brunt of my emotional venting—but to her, it just felt like I was testing her patience. In response, she would often shut down a conversation before it had even started, with one of two responses ready: the "I already know everything" one or the "Is this all you ever talk about?" one. I hated both of them. Looking back on it, I probably did talk about transition an awful lot, but I needed somebody to vent to. This is going to sound really sad, but I've never really had many friends that I could open up to, so a lot of the time my mum had to fill those shoes. After a while I realized she wasn't the best person to have casual transition chats with, so I turned to the internet and eventually support groups for those conversations.

My mum is a medical geek, so throughout my transition we bonded over navigating the health care system. Regardless of whether she'd accepted it yet, if I felt like I absolutely had to get on testosterone and have surgery, there was no way she was going

to let me do it alone. She was around for every bump and hiccup on the road. She came with me for my first blood tests, read up on anything I was going to get done, and basically made sure all the professionals were doing their jobs. I did have to tell her to stay outside during my first T shot though; I couldn't deal with her being in the room while I exposed my butt cheek to a total stranger! That made her a little sad, but she still got the pleasure of watching me limp out of the room clutching my ass in pain, so she didn't miss much.

If anything, I think my transliness forced me and my mum to get closer, and her gradually increasing support brought us together after those rough teenage years.

These days, my mum likes to look on the lighter side of transition, making man jokes in an attempt to get me to lift heavy bags or eat giant portions of her cooking. She's a typical mum of a young man: she pulls up my sagging pants, opens my curtains, and tucks in the labels of my shirts. That aside, it's pretty weird how alike we are, from our awkward lanky bodies to our horrible potty mouths. Sometimes it's like we're the same person. One thing's for sure: she's now a shining example of what a parent of a trans child should be. Proud, supportive, and

I was terrified to tell him I was trans.

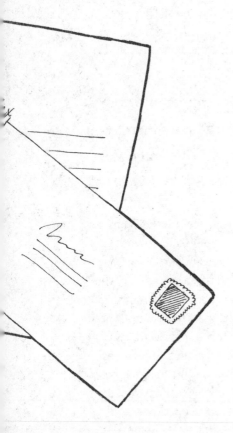

knowledgeable, and as tough as nails when it comes to taking care of her kid.

Things with my dad worked a bit differently. To be honest, I was terrified to tell him I was trans, but I knew I couldn't leave too long a gap between my mum finding out and him finding out. He's not an easy person to read and I really had no idea how he'd react to me coming out. His accepting response to my sexuality a few years earlier had blown me away, and he was generally okay with the more masculine way I presented, but we'd already clashed a few times because I never wanted to try out typically girly activities or clothes. Trying to predict his reaction was impossible, so just a few months after I had given my mum her letter, I decided it was time to bite the bullet and tackle Dad.

His reaction to my transition was so hard to deal with in the moment, but it's been one of the most satisfying things to see develop over time. As with my mum, I officially came out to him through a letter when I was seventeen. I say "officially" because he'd heard the gist of it from reading the letter I wrote to my mum a few months earlier, but I still needed to tell him myself. I typed up another letter but left it on my computer for weeks. I even posted it anonymously on the internet to get people's opinions on things I could rephrase or edit—I wanted to give him the best chance of understanding right away.

I waited for a while until I had the courage to finally print it one day and leave it under his computer keyboard before I went to college.

I actually recently found it in a drawer, so with his permission I'd like to reproduce it here.

Dad,

Last Christmas, I wrote Mum a letter—and I know you read it too, but we never spoke about it and since then that's all I've wanted. I just want to be honest and I really need your support because...well, you're my dad. I guess I'm just scared. Scared of talking to you, scared of what you'll think of me...just scared of everything.

The letter to Mum was basically about my gender and how I was questioning. It's been like this for three years, and every day it gets harder to live with myself while having this massive problem hanging over my head. The black and white of it is that I feel male. Mentally I see myself as male. I've never felt female and everything about being a girl just makes me cringe and hurt. Hearing people say she, *Birth name,* her, daughter, girls…It just makes me so uncomfortable and I genuinely find it hard to respond.

I'm in a lot of pain living in this body. I find the idea of swimming daunting, meeting new people is a huge fear, I don't have the confidence to apply for a job, my period is a monthly reminder that my body doesn't match who I am inside, and I can't even bear the thought of going out in public with my own family in case someone mistakes me for a boy. I wish I had been born physically male so that I would never have had to write this stupid letter. I feel humiliated and like a disgrace to our family.

This is definitely not something that happened overnight; it's been like this for so long. Like I said, for the past three years I've been trying to come to terms with it myself. At first I accepted the fact that I was still young and that my feelings could change, but now I know what I want and I can't see my future any other way.

I can understand if this is hard for you, and I realize that this will be difficult for everyone—but trust me, I wouldn't choose feeling this way if I could. I also

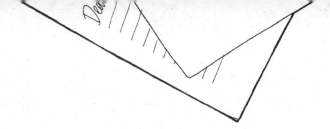

know that this isn't something that can be sorted out right away. It's all pretty medical-based, a lot of which can't even happen until I'm eighteen. I just don't want you to worry and I want you to know that I'm well aware of everything that comes with this and the effect it could have on my future.

There's more, but you can get a feel of it from this. At the time, I was in my third week of college, which meant for three weeks I had been surrounded by people using the correct name and pronouns. I had wanted to start college being my authentic self.

Despite my puny body and ridiculously high voice, they all saw me as a guy and there was no way I wanted anything ruining that.

I was terrified that one day my dad would meet my new friends or talk to my new teachers and use the wrong name. The people that I was closest to knew I was trans, but I still didn't want to be put in that awkward position. I knew I had to tell him what was going on and how people referred to me.

By lunchtime the day I left the letter under his keyboard, I still hadn't heard anything from him. So surrounded by my friends in the college cafeteria, all of us staring at my phone, I texted him where to find the letter and told him to read it. After a long pause, my phone lit up with a message from him. My dad's never been great at full-blown text conversations, but I could tell that this time he really didn't know what to say. When I prompted him for more of a reaction, asking what he thought, he replied saying that we'd speak later when I got home.

By the time I had made it through the day, the adrenaline from him finding the letter was gone and all I was left with was anxiety and fear.

When we were finally at home together, I explained that I had introduced myself at college as Alex and that I wanted to change my name and get professional help. I kept trying to reinforce that even though I wanted to change my name, I was still me.

I was always so scared of opening up to him like this and I have no idea why. It was such an irrational fear because he never exploded with rage like I thought he would. He's more of a silent type, which can be equally scary because you never know what he's thinking. As it turned out, his initial reaction was disheartening. When I told him I didn't feel like a girl, he responded, "But that's how you were born." All kinds of things were said by both him and me. He said he didn't "agree with it," and that he didn't think he could ever see me as his son. I accused him of not caring and told him I hated coming home because

It wasn't pretty, but that was the reality of the situation.

nobody respected me like they did at college.

It wasn't pretty, but that was the reality of the situation back then. Lots of harsh words were said on both sides, but everything was necessary because it was honest feelings that were being aired. Despite the friction, just the fact that I didn't have to hide who I was made a world of difference to my confidence. Suddenly I didn't have to pretend anymore: I could put my boxer shorts in the washing pile instead of sneaking them into the machine; I could wear shorts with my hairy legs on display; I could get my hair cut a little bit shorter. I felt free.

That silver lining didn't last long though. After the letter, my dad and I rarely spoke about my transition because it would always result in tears—on my part, that is! It was very hard to talk to him about things—while he'd never shit on what I'd say, it was very emotionally draining to open myself up. The conversation would end and I wouldn't feel like any progress had been made at all.

MY dad slowly STARTED to come AROUND.

That didn't stop me from trying to talk about it once in a while though. Sometimes dysphoria would hit and I'd be so low that it was impossible to hide it, so when my dad asked what was wrong, I'd just tell him. I thought my best chance at getting him to understand why I was transitioning was to be as honest as possible.

After a few years of me just living life and trying to be myself, it seemed that my dad slowly started to come around. One of the biggest steps forward happened on Transgender Day of Remembrance back in 2014. I traveled up the country to visit Lancashire University with my boyfriend Jake; he sang songs for the audience and I did a speech that was streamed live on the internet. I mentioned it to my parents but didn't expect them to tune in, so when I read a text from my dad after the talk saying I had done a good job, it left me speechless.

From that point on, I think he respected my decision to transition; he realized how important it was to me because of the words I'd spoken.

We didn't sit around together knitting little trans flags or picking him out a shirt that read "I <3 MY TRANS SON," but he was cool with it.

I began attending appointments at a gender identity clinic in Exeter when I was eighteen, in 2015, and I remained in the mindset that keeping my parents up to date would keep them close. This definitely worked out well—I remember calling my dad and telling him all about my first appointment as soon as I walked out of the clinic.

Being really open about my desire for hormones also earned me more of his support.

When I was suffering in the wait leading up to testosterone, he'd always sit and hear me out. After one particularly depressing visit to the clinic, when they told me how long the wait list was for the specialist doctors, I came home really upset. I curled up on my bed and cried. Hard. It was one of the first times I allowed my parents to see me in a very raw state of dysphoria. Nothing I said was filtered, I just sat there feeling defeated with words of self-hate, despair, and anger falling messily out of my mouth. Both my parents stood by me, trying to be encouraging. It couldn't have been easy.

After seeing my slow medical progression and the effort I was putting in to move forward, my parents both started using neutral pronouns and avoided using my birth name, making me a lot more comfortable around the house. I can still remember the first time I realized they were making a conscious effort not to offend me; even my boyfriend commented on it.

I found myself stunned with how fast things were changing. In February 2016 I was getting really close to getting my first testosterone shot. The doctor called me to cancel a vital blood test, which was the last thing standing between me and hormones. It left me in pieces and I was hysterical. To my surprise, my dad picked up the phone right away. Through his dogged persistence and stern tone, I got a blood test the next day. He used different pronouns all the way through the call (no doubt leaving the receptionist a little confused), but he called me Alex and he fought to help me get the hormones that meant so much to me.

The year 2017 was the start of something amazing, as not only did my dad start calling me Alex more frequently, but he even called me his son.

I vividly remember a conversation over text five years ago, when he said he didn't know if he could ever call me that. I wanted him to call me his son so badly. I wanted to be accepted into the "man circle" of the house. My mum and sister were the girls, my dad was the man, and I was the... Alex. It was pretty lonely. So when I finally heard him accept me into the guy group, it was incredible.

He was there being his goofy self while I was in a hospital bed.

My dad has changed so much. I never for a second thought that he'd be supportive when I went through surgery, but he was there being his goofy self while I was in a hospital bed. The other day he actually pointed out my stubble and suggested that I moisturize after shaving. WHAT?! AM I EVEN ALIVE RIGHT NOW?! He even pulls my mum's trick, telling me to help him move furniture and that it should be easy "because of all that extra testosterone" in my body.

It's a wonderful thing knowing that my dad's there if I need him, and much like how I feel with my mum, I hope I haven't caused him too much pain. In fact, my experience with my parents has shaped the way I give advice not only to parents of LGBTQ+ youth, but to the young people themselves. It's key to remember that as much as your transition is about you and your struggle, other people in your life will be affected too. It used to really get to me when people complained about how hard my transition was for them, because in my eyes nobody was

Alex

WHAT?!
am i
even
ALIVE right
now?!

hurting more than me. As hard as it was to think about anything other than my dysphoria, I wish I had been more understanding of how difficult it was for my parents during the worst times. I wanted them to support me immediately, but in reality it takes time to get used to seeing someone in a different light.

That's always the first thing I say to someone when they think their parents don't care or are transphobic: give them time.

Transitioning is always going to be a big deal to your parents and they're never going to respond with "Oh wow! I'm so glad my child is trapped in a body that makes them feel horrible!" A lot of parents react negatively out of fear or miseducation, so it's best to come out armed with information to help them understand, or at least be open to answering their questions yourself. It's also important to remember that there's a high chance you've known you're trans for a lot longer than they've known you are. While they've only just landed on step one, you're miles ahead with loads more thinking time and information behind you, so it might take them a while to catch up.

The best advice I can give to someone coming out to or dealing with unsupportive parents is to just give them time and be open in how you feel.

Chances are that they're not going to be unsupportive forever, no matter how far gone you think they are. There was a time (and I have video proof of this) when I wanted to just give up on all hope that my parents would ever come around. But you know what? I persevered and kept them as close as possible until they got it. How are they supposed to learn about your life or see you being happy if you don't let them in?

While it's important to know that not all coming out stories are stressful or negative, it does sometimes go that way.

You need to make sure that you're in a safe position to deal with the consequences of a more negative response. If you're young and you think your parents will have a bad reaction, the best thing to do is wait until you've moved out or have the means to. You don't want to be kicked out without any money to get your own place or be stuck in a bad environment. As important as being yourself is, being kicked out or being made to feel terrible is going to make the path to happiness even harder.

If coming out to others, such as friends or a partner, doesn't go well, it's important to remember that you can't let anyone hold you back from being happy, no matter what. If transitioning is something you need to do and you put it on hold because of someone else, you will regret it. Why live your life being unhappy just because somebody can't deal with change? If someone is really against you transitioning and is threatening you in any way, they're selfish and not worth it. You need people in your life who are supportive of your happiness.

As for siblings, you might find that they have a more positive reaction, especially if they're younger. When she was just eleven years old, I found that my sister was really accepting—my new name rolled off her tongue with ease. Hollie impressed me so much that I made multiple videos with her on my YouTube channel to show that coming out to young kids isn't damaging or a negative influence, as some horrible people out there would have you believe.

I think kids are just naturally more open-minded, especially if you're patient and allow them to ask you questions.

Older people can surprise you too, though. My extended family found out I was trans when my uncle stumbled across my YouTube channel, and their response was amazing. My nan called me to say that I didn't need to worry and that the rest of the family had been told. She said that she might not be great at remembering my name "because she's old," but that it wasn't out of disrespect and that everyone loved me very much. A few days after her phone call, I got a letter in the mail.

Hi Alex,

We all thought we would write you a letter, just to say we are very proud of you being able to find your path in life.

It must have been very difficult for you over the years, but now you are becoming the person you want to be. We will always support you, whatever your choices may be throughout your life. We completely understand why you may have felt uneasy letting the family know, and now we are aware hopefully this is a small weight off your shoulders.

Looking forward to seeing you soon.

If you need anything at all, or to chat, or to come and visit, you are always welcome.

Your family (friends)

It was a short read, but I think it's the best reaction anyone could ask for from family, especially those of an older generation. I hadn't told the rest of the family for a number of reasons, the first being that

I didn't know how. We all live far apart and we rarely get together, so it would have been a little weird to call them up one day and say, "Hi, I know we haven't spoken in six months but just letting you know...I'm a man." Besides, I figured that what they didn't know couldn't hurt them; they wouldn't worry about me, nor would they grill my parents for not telling them.

I'm really lucky that, even though we're not exactly close, some of my extended family have been really good about my transliness.

Recently the whole family got together for my parents' wedding. I was completely blown away by everyone calling me Alex and the fact that they didn't make a huge fuss over my changes on testosterone. My uncle was particularly amazing. He didn't bat an eye when he used my name and he even went in for a handshake instead of a hug, which was probably his way of using a more "masculine" greeting than the bear hugs he'd given before. As sweet as the gesture was, I couldn't help but shake his hand and pull him into a hug anyway to say goodbye. I'm just an affectionate guy, and...well...he's family!

In short, the early days of coming out can seem a little rough, but you have to try to see things from your family's perspective. A lot of parents

It can be quite a shock to see someone they love become physically different.

need time, almost to mourn the loss of the child they thought they had, before they can open up to the new person they see before them. Of course, a trans person is always the same at their core. But to close friends and family, it can be quite a shock to see someone they love become physically different, even though to the trans person their new appearance is just how they felt all along. It's like a gardener planting what they think is a tomato seed, watching it grow while tending to it every day and building up a vision of its future. The gardener nurtures it, all the time imagining everything they'll be able to do with the tomato once it's grown. When they discover that it was never a tomato seed, but actually a pepper, they have to step back and reevaluate everything they'd thought while the plant was growing. It's a pretty weird analogy, but it kind of works. Parents might think they've lost something when their child comes out as trans, but the reality is that the kid is going to turn out just as great as their parents always thought, just a little different.

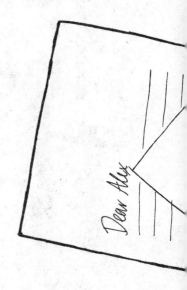

SO
sometimes
you HAVE
to
celebrate
the LITTLE
things.

Acceptance and respect definitely take time and come in stages, so sometimes you have to celebrate the little things; the chances are, they're leading up to something great. I'd encourage anyone frustrated by family to give them time.

Don't shut them out, no matter how much you think it might help.

Keep your family involved in your normal day-to-day life as well as sitting them down for serious talks; you can't expect someone to accept you if they barely know you. I'm very lucky to now feel respected and accepted by my folks, even if it was a bumpy ride. Honestly, my family is a prime example of why you should never give up hope on yours. One day, things might fall into place and they will surprise you.

10

HELLO! MY NAME IS...

I wanted something more masculine.

I came out to my friends as casually as possible near the end of school, when I was sixteen. I was too scared at first to use the term "transgender," so I dipped a toe in the water and described myself as having "gender issues." Nobody was really that surprised, and some of my friends even said, "Oh, it all makes sense now!"

With a supportive friend group, it didn't take long before the question of a new "male" name came up to make me feel more comfortable. My birth name wasn't terrible, but I wanted something more masculine that I felt proud to use and that didn't hold memories of a time pre-transition. One summer day out with my buddies in town, I downloaded a baby names app to my phone and we all sat in a circle thinking about what my new name should be.

We went through popular names of 1995, my birth year, because as much as I'd love to be called "Zyther" or something just as contemporary and obscure, I wanted my parents to actually use my new name eventually. We must have gone through hundreds of names, but the main ones that stuck out were Alex, Tom, Damien, Ben, Kaden, and Zac. The first name I really liked was Alex, and as soon as it was suggested, everyone else agreed too—with the exception of one trans lady who had Alex as her chosen name, who insisted that I couldn't be called

My old name was a statement of my time living as female.

the same thing. As stupid as that was, I went along with it, picking Kaden as my chosen name because I thought it sounded cool. I have no idea if that girl still uses that name, but I sure as hell didn't stick with Kaden—I switched back to Alex within about three months.

I told my parents the name I wanted to start using when I first came out as trans to them, but it took years for it to stick. Once I'd announced my name change, whenever someone used my birth name, it hurt like a burn that would linger for days. It felt like all the work and pain I had put into transitioning had been undone with one word. My old name was a statement of my time living as female, and it infuriated me to hear it.

Along with my new name came new pronouns. Since I was now identifying as a man, I wasn't comfortable with people saying "she" or "her" when talking about me, so whenever I heard someone say it, I'd quickly respond "he" or "his" to make it clear that the

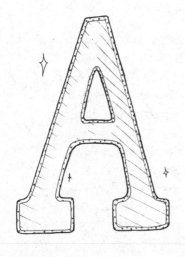

wrong pronoun upset me just as much as hearing my birth name. I don't think there was a particular video on YouTube where I said, "Hi guys, from now on I'd like you to call me Alex." Instead, it was a gradual process—and for a long time, my YouTube username was still my birth name, so it wasn't like it was hard to find.

My only YouTube regret is using my birth name at the beginning, not that I could have helped that.

It still haunts me to this day; luckily, YouTube allows me to "blacklist" certain words used in comments so they need to be approved before they can be displayed publicly. The list of words I currently get flagged includes my birth name (including all the different ways it can be spelled) and an array of homophobic or transphobic language. It's an easy way of cleaning up the comments section from trolls and keeps me from being hurt by harmful speech.

I was still in school when I came up with Alex, and it took a few years for me to start changing my name officially. You can change your name with parental consent before eighteen, but my parents refused to sign the paperwork. They didn't do it to hurt me; they did it so that when I changed it myself I'd know it was all down to me. It was a life lesson about having responsibility and working for the things you want. There are no strict laws on how to change your name in the UK; some places simply accept a signed piece of paper from yourself and a witness if it has the correct legal wording. However, I've heard of people having a difficult time if it doesn't look official enough, because the laws are hazy. For some peace of mind and to feel a little more legitimate, I went through an "official" deed poll website that had a video testimony from a famous news presenter on the front page. I paid some money, got sent some deed polls with blank spaces for my details, and sat down at a desk in college with my tutor there to countersign as a witness. The certificate I got in the mail featured a stamp, watermarked paper, and a serial number (I don't even know if it means anything), and it cost me £20 (about $25).

Technically it wasn't any more legally binding than what I could have done for free, but it did probably help me avoid too many suspiciously raised eyebrows.

When I sat down to complete the forms, I still wasn't sure what I wanted to change my middle names to (obviously I was extremely prepared . . .). My original middle names were Michelle and Bernadette; Michelle is my mum's name and Bernadette is a saint. I didn't care much about the saint, but I still

wanted my mum to be a part of my name. Eventually I settled on using her maiden name, Ashby.
"Alex Ashby Bertie" still sounded a little weird, so I shortened it to just "Ash." It gets my mum in there and still sounds cool. Win-win!

It must have taken about a year to get all my documents changed to my new name; many places required me to send off my deed poll and other forms of ID before they made the change, and others made finding information about registering a new name really hard.

It wasn't hard to change my name in the UK, but it can be more challenging in other countries. If you want to change your name legally, make sure to do your research!

When mail started coming through the door with my new name, it really started to hit home to my parents that this was all permanent.

Before then, my mum had found it quite difficult to use the correct name, which I think was down to the fact that she would say different things depending on who she was talking to. She'd try her best to say Alex when talking to me, but it was obvious she was still using my old name to everyone else, given how frequently she'd slip up. When I first asked my dad to

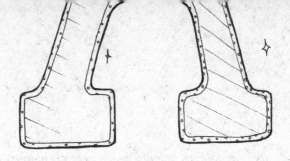

use my new name, he didn't say no exactly, but he said he would always see me as what he named me. Hearing someone refuse an important request is frustrating, because it makes you feel like everything you're fighting for within your transition is worthless.

At first, I didn't feel like either of my parents cared enough.

When they used my birth name and female pronouns, it felt like they weren't even trying. In their defense, I now understand how difficult it must be to change the way you address someone (especially your own child) after knowing them for so long.

My sister, Hollie, started using the correct name pretty much the second I came out to her, so she was a great example to both my parents and really helped to normalize "Alex" being said around the house. Another big step forward was when my official name change was complete—having an official ID in the correct name was really affirming. Still, it took until I was nineteen for my mum to consistently call me Alex. Today, she always uses the correct name. It took a long time and a lot of correcting to get here, but she really does understand how that mistake makes me feel. Just the other day, she compared the use of my old name to swearing—she really gets it now.

Over time, my dad stopped using any pronouns and avoided either name. That was pretty awkward, because whenever he was speaking, he'd leave a silent gap where my name or pronouns should be, instead just gesturing toward me. But as weird as it was, it was also pretty amazing.

It was a huge sign that he was starting to understand how the wrong name or pronouns made me feel.

Going on testosterone really kicked things up a notch for my dad, because the more I changed physically, the more I noticed him getting things right in speech. I'm not sure if it was my increased masculinity that made things easier or just coincidence that it clicked around the same time. I don't know, and to be honest I don't care: I will never tire of hearing him say my name.

I found that how lenient I was about people getting my name wrong depended on who they were. For example, if they were a friend or someone who followed me online and happened to know my birth name, there was no excuse for using it. With my parents, I had to be more patient.

My birth name still haunts me to this day and makes me feel very uncomfortable when I hear it, even if it's being used to refer to someone else. I get this feeling of being disconnected from my body; it's like I try to mentally remove myself from the situation. The closest thing I can liken it to is those crazy stories you hear about people who've been under anesthesia or in a coma, unconscious but somehow looking down at themselves in the hospital bed.

When going through the process of changing your name, it's a case of picking your battles.

Not everyone is going to get it right away (or maybe even ever), but you have to appreciate those who try and prioritize the people who matter the most. I'd also recommend that if you're close to your parents or you have the ability to talk about names with them, you should ask them what they think you should change your name to or what they would have called you if you were born the gender you identify as now. You might be pleasantly surprised by the help, come to a compromise, or it might just make them feel good that you're letting them into this part of your life—even if you don't take their suggestions. It's a pretty odd thing to pick a name for yourself. Not many people get to do it, and I'm not going to lie—it's pretty fun, like naming your character in a video game.

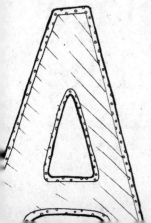

11

BEING STEALTH
AT COLLEGE

College was
the place
I truly felt like
"Alex Bertie."

My first day of college as a tiny, fluffy sixteen-year-old was a huge deal for me because I was able to introduce myself however I wanted. For the first time, I could be myself without anyone asking too many questions or judging me based on rumors. Having had a pretty terrible school experience, I'd decided that college was going to be different. This time I'd go in confident (even if it was fake!), go out of my way to be friendly and, most importantly, I'd be myself. That might all sound cliché, but it definitely worked. By the end of my first day, I had a group of guy friends who were everything I'd ever wanted. They all had similar interests to me and were accepting of LGBTQ+ things, but also had this "bro banter" that I'd never encountered before, which helped my confidence and thickened my shell.

Everyone was friendly and as long as you weren't an asshole, people talked to you no matter how different you seemed. When I think of the people there, I'm always brought back to a long hallway where we'd all sit shoulder-to-shoulder on the floor waiting for classes.

Sometimes there'd be total silence, the only sound being raindrops hitting the tin roof, and other days the hallway was filled with laughter.

Being transgender didn't make a difference to my time there—at least, not once the first couple of weeks had passed. On my first day, I heard my birth name called during class registration. Horrified, I responded by ducking my head and trying to say yes without anyone seeing the word come out of my mouth. Then and there I decided to tell some college staff that I was trans. It meant I could get my name changed in the system and also just made life easier when potentially difficult-to-explain things came up. It ended up being a great move because my tutor Ellie was incredibly helpful and supportive.

Words can't describe the gratitude I feel for Ellie—I can only hope that there are more teachers out there who take their students' well-being so seriously. A lot of trans kids feel alone and may be suffering either in or outside of school, so having someone genuine

Being "stealth" refers to people not knowing your trans status.

they can put trust in would do a whole lot of good.

Recently I asked Ellie if she'd ever said anything to any other staff about my transition. She told me that she briefed them all (including admin!) on my situation, and told them to ask her if they had any questions or concerns. She also gave all the staff an info sheet to help educate them about transgender matters. It was because of this great work that I was able to be stealth throughout my time at college.

Being "stealth" refers to people not knowing your trans status, instead using your preferred name and pronouns with no knowledge of your past.

Being stealth meant that college was the place I truly felt like Alex Bertie—the response at home still wasn't great at that time. By choosing not to tell people, I wasn't hiding who I was—just who I had been. It meant that 70 percent of

i wasn't
HIDING
WHO i
was.

my week consisted of being referred to with the correct name and pronouns, which was so affirming for me and added to my confidence as a man. I did tell one of my close friends, Sean, that I was trans.

He simply replied "Cool!" and continued talking.

Occasionally I'd need to formally come out to other students because they'd found my YouTube channel, but the best way to deal with it was just to be honest and relaxed. I found that if I reacted in a hostile way, the conversation just became more awkward and the other student stopped taking in what I was telling them.

I attended college for a total of four years from the ages of sixteen to twenty, studying two different courses. My first course was a level three diploma in art and design, which was where I found my passion for graphics. I came out of that with the highest grade possible (if you work hard, you're allowed to brag!) and then started a higher national diploma (HND) in graphic design. I chose that instead of going to university, but HNDs didn't seem very popular among other people my age in the UK. I still don't understand why—doing a higher course at college is cheaper, one year shorter, and doesn't involve writing a huge dissertation. I mean, I guess life is getting back at me for that last one with this book, but there you go!

The HND was really different than my first two years. Level three had been easy because everyone was the same age as me and we all had similar interests, but the new HND group was a lot older. I was pretty much the youngest person in the room, with people being over twenty-five years older than me in some cases. It took a year for me to open up and find friends within the class—though to be fair, it probably didn't help that I sat in the corner of the room most of the time!

My nerves in that class made me realize something I don't talk about often but that is probably obvious to everyone I meet.

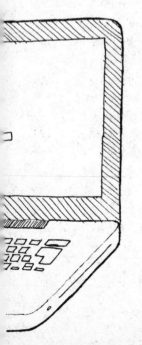

I discovered that I was far more introverted than I thought and that I struggle in daunting social situations. When talking to people that I feel are "higher up" than me in some way, I just babble, stutter, and fall over my words out of nervousness. It's the same with YouTubers I look up to or people at work. It's odd: I'm fine when I feel comfortable, such as when I'm talking to followers at events or people at trans social groups.

I came out to my class after our teacher gave us a project to create a website portfolio for our work. I decided to combine my art with my video-making about trans issues and put them both on the site.

It was a huge weight off my shoulders and allowed me to interact with my classmates because I finally felt like I wasn't hiding a part of me.

From then on, I actually made some friends—and I was able to center my final project around a trans topic, which was amazing.

We were allowed to design anything we wanted, so I chose to develop the graphics for a mobile app called "All Things Trans." I designed everything, even animating the app as if it was being used. It was a great project because the writing portion was so easy—I didn't have to do a lot of research because I already knew it all!

It had always been my goal to start hormone treatment before finishing college, because I didn't think I could face the adult world without actually looking like an adult. After years of being in the health care system, just a month before I finished college, I finally started testosterone when I was twenty. The class never got to hear my voice break, so I'm waiting for the day we have a reunion and my voice BLOWS THEIR MINDS!

12

YOUTH GROUP SUPPORT

It's nice to know that there's a group of people I can turn to if I need support.

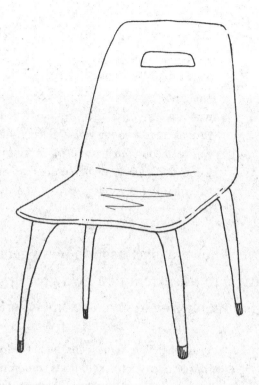

One of the best things to ever happen to me in the years seeking hormone treatment was that I joined a trans social group. I found my first trans youth group through my tutor Ellie, and being able to talk to other trans kids in person really helped me through a lot of issues. We helped each other lift our spirits and just enjoyed each other's company. The group gave us a safe space to be ourselves just once a week. Since all the group members were local and at different stages in their transition, it also gave me a good idea of how our local health care system responded to trans patients.

We'd meet every Thursday at 3 p.m., and Ellie would let me finish my college day early to be with them. The group was led by a youth worker named Dan, who was just finishing his course to be fully qualified. He was quite a young guy, and from the beginning was really open to learning more about transitioning; within a few weeks he had more than enough to go on to structure our conversations and activities to really help our group.

I've never known a cis person to be so genuinely supportive, to the extent that he'd give up so much of his own time for free to give us somewhere to go.

We managed to film videos, be in the local paper, make podcasts, travel to trans conferences around the UK, and even talk to school kids about trans issues at a diversity event. We were really making a difference. The group kept doubling, with more and more members joining of all different gender identities. We'd read somewhere that statistically there were more trans women than men, but for some reason our group had barely any trans ladies. I really wish I had met more trans women my age while I was in the group because I would have learned so much more.

I ended up leaving the group when I turned nineteen because the newer members joining were all pretty

WE were really MAKING A difference.

young (ages thirteen to fifteen), and the conversations deviated quite a lot from trans topics. The membership cap of the group was technically twenty-four, but it was pretty disheartening knowing that without older members, I'd eventually have nobody to relate to. I'm really grateful for the friendships I made there and that Dan led the group so well, but I ended up growing out of it.

During the next two years, I didn't attend any groups at all. I'm not great about meeting new people or being the new guy in any situation, so finding a new group was really unappealing.

I was also going through a hard time during that period—I was on a ridiculously long wait list at my gender identity clinic before going on hormones, so I'm kind of glad I got to distance myself from everything related to transitioning. That's why it was a blessing that, after a few months on T, I heard that Dan had left the youth group and was starting his own trans group for members over eighteen.

It's called Communi-t and takes place every other Friday. I'm not going to lie, sometimes I go months without attending a meeting—but it's nice to know that there's a group of people I can turn to if I need support. The atmosphere is a lot more positive and adult too; we don't just sit around in a room feeling sorry for ourselves and hating on the long wait lists, because let's face it: you can do that alone on your own time. Instead, we spend one hour at the local LGBTQ+ center, where we play silly games and introduce ourselves, then the next two hours in a public space like a bar or a café.

As much as I sometimes hate leaving the house to spend time in a public area, it's not so bad when people similar to you are around.

I feel a lot safer going into a place that I don't know with the group, because nobody is stupid enough to harass somebody with a group of twenty people behind them! I don't think anybody would actually do that in my area, but I still have the irrational fear because I always feel so vulnerable.

Communi-t has restored my faith in social groups, and I'm now a strong believer in the need to have some sort of support network behind you. Transitioning is a huge thing and can feel lonely if you don't have the support of your family or friends. That's why a social group is a blessing, because everyone is in the same boat! It's also a great way to get support without pressure or obligations. With friendships, you have to work

EVERYONE is IN the Same BOAT.

to maintain a connection, but a group is there whenever you need it. No matter how long I leave it between attending meetings, when I'm back at group, it's like no time has passed at all.

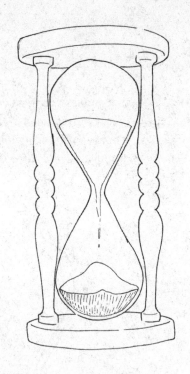

13

STARTING MY PHYSICAL TRANSITION

All that matters is being your true self.

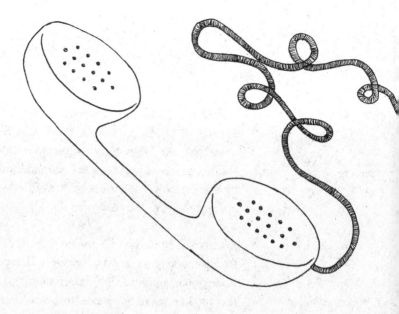

I didn't start my physical journey for years. In the UK, you can't access treatments like hormones before the age of seventeen without parental consent, and I didn't see the point in getting my name in the system unless I knew hormones were on the horizon. And even when I turned seventeen, I wanted to give my parents the chance to come around and support me through it. Eventually, when I turned eighteen in 2014, I decided to go ahead and begin the process despite not having their full support. It was a tough decision, but knowing that wait times could be incredibly long, I hoped they would come around by the time I was on hormones.

I decided to go through the public National Health Service (NHS) because I would never have been able to pay for it myself for the rest of my life. Hormones would cost far more, surgery would be too expensive, and the regular psychotherapy appointments would really add up.

Just getting a referral to a gender identity clinic was a struggle, due to a lot of my local general practioners having no experience with trans patients. The first time I opened up to a doctor was a disaster. I remember going into the room nervously thinking about what I was going to say over and over to make sure I didn't miss anything.

Once inside, I explained that I thought I was transgender and proceeded to tell my whole life story up until that point.

When I'd finished, the doctor told me she had no idea how to help me—and unfortunately I didn't know what the process was for trans patients, so I couldn't help steer her either. Instead, I left her to do some research.

Months later, I received a referral to a mental health clinic. I might not have known everything about the pathway for trans patients, but I was sure a mental health clinic wasn't going to help me. To receive

The first time I opened up to a doctor was a disaster.

such a response after opening myself up like that was so disheartening. I felt unbelievably defeated, and it took about six months before I found the courage to try again.

I couldn't take having to deal with my dysphoria anymore and started spiraling into a really bad place mentally. I was very erratic—sometimes I coped fine for ages, but then a small thing could happen, like my dad using the wrong name or me looking at certain parts of my body, and it would send me into self-destruct mode.

My boyfriend Jake was really the one who dragged me into the health care system again. On one of my bad days, Jake encouraged me to book an appointment and try once more. When the appointment date to see my family doctor arrived, I went in armed with official public health care guidelines for trans patients, detailing everything required from my doctor. To make things even clearer, I also found the address and contact information of the nearest gender identity clinic to take with me.

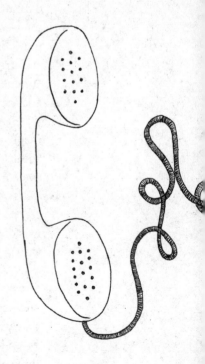

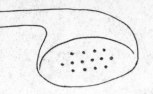

In my eyes, the appointment went well from start to finish. I went in, gave a clear explanation of why I felt transgender, answered her questions, and told her exactly which clinic I wanted to be referred to.

She even told me she had experience dealing with trans patients, so I thought nothing could go wrong. It did. She ignored everything I gave her and once again referred me to the same mental health clinic as the previous doctor.

Furious, I demanded to speak to her on the phone and firmly told her that I was not required to go through a mental health clinic for an assessment, and that I would have to do one anyway when I got to the specialist clinic. Ignoring everything I said and the evidence I had provided, the doctor stuck with her decision and the call ended. This time there was no stopping me. I was determined to get on hormones even if I had to go through every goddamn doctor in the United Kingdom.

So yet again, I booked another appointment with another general practioner. Guess what? The third time was the charm. He listened to me and finally I was referred to the clinic I'd hoped for. It took another three months to get my first appointment there, which was with a psychotherapist. She explained that throughout my transition, I'd have ongoing appointments with her to talk about anything I wanted.

The first three appointments I had with her spanned four months, and by my third appointment I had completed the assessment phase. I was diagnosed as a transgender man.

The initial sessions with her were extremely personal, digging up lots of things from my childhood—including those I would never have thought could have been related to my transition. Things like the fact my mum worked a lot during my early childhood, leaving me predominantly with my dad. At times I could almost see through her questions, with the phrase "strong male influence at early age" flashing through my mind. Fortunately, I'd spent a lot of time leading up to my appointment putting myself in a good mental place, which really paid off. Not too much earlier, I wouldn't have been able to talk about my parents without breaking down, but after I'd worked on my mental state by making YouTube videos, delving into the most painful details of my life didn't cause me any problems. I think it confused my therapist a bit—she actually commented on how my responses seemed very

i FOUND the invasive questions kind of offensive and IRRELEVANT.

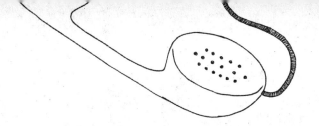

thought-through, even calculated. To her, it might have seemed like I had rehearsed my replies, but the reality was that I had spoken about my experiences so much in my online videos that it just felt like I was regurgitating information to another stranger.

At the time, I found the invasive questions kind of offensive and irrelevant. But over the past few years I've come to understand more about why the professionals have to be 100 percent sure that medical transition is the right thing for you. It's quite simple really: hormones and surgery can have irreversible effects on the body, and they don't want to be responsible if you ever feel like you've made a mistake and need to detransition.

I can already feel hundreds of trans people rolling their eyes reading this. Detransitioning can be a frustrating, touchy subject.

Stories of people detransitioning are often seen as a bit of a plague on the trans community. Not because detransitioning is bad, but because the media jumps on those rare stories as soon as they hear about them, making them seem more frequent than they are and portraying all trans people as confused individuals who don't know what they're getting

Discovering and figuring out your gender identity can be incredibly confusing.

themselves into. It's a big factor in why the question that trans people so often get asked when they come out is "What if you change your mind?"

To explain, detransitioning is when someone goes through the steps of transitioning, such as starting hormones and perhaps even having surgery, and then later realizes they made a mistake. They come off the hormones and try to reverse the changes that have already happened. Some parts of a transition are pretty easy to reverse, while others, such as a voice break, are often permanent. Discovering and figuring out your gender identity can be incredibly confusing. Taking the brave step of coming out and working to get hormones is hard enough—I can't imagine then having to tell people that it was all a mistake.

I really wish doctors could just zap your brain to see if you need to transition, to stop people ending up in that horrible situation. There are some people who have known that they're trans their whole life, but

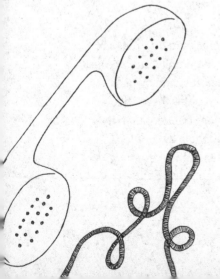

plenty of others figure things out a little later on—
and then there are people who feel stuck and just
don't know if transitioning is right for them.

Over the last few years, the discussion surrounding
gender identity has progressed quickly and I think
it will really help people who are deciding whether
to medically transition. Gender is starting to be
recognized as more of a spectrum than just as two
opposite possibilities: male or female. Some people
feel totally male, some feel totally female, some are
a bit of both, some are 75 percent one way, and
others are neither. This greater understanding is
an amazing thing, and the sooner professionals in
clinics are on board with it, the better the treatment
options will be.

The important thing to remember is that life
goes on.

No matter who you are, how you identify, whether
you're detransitioning, just starting hormones, or
finally getting to a point where you're happy,
it's possible to have a happy, normal life just
like everyone else.

All that matters is being your true self. It's important
that we take care of each other. Trans people want

respect and acceptance, so it's only right we give the same to those detransitioning.

It was learning more about detransitioning that put everything I had to go through into perspective. *Oh, so that's why I needed all those psychotherapy appointments. That's why they needed to know everything about my life.* The people at the gender identity clinic asked all those invasive questions for a reason. They just wanted to figure everything out and help me make sure I was making the right decision. It's thanks to this very thorough process of evaluation at the gender identity clinic that detransitioning is so rare, as any doubts will rise to the surface there.

Personally, my heart was set on transitioning very soon after I found out I could, and I've never had any second thoughts. I can't imagine being anything other than a man.

After the third session with the psychotherapist, I continued to have appointments with her while being on the wait list to see the clinic doctor. This doctor would look at my assessment and make the call about whether I was suitable for hormone therapy and surgery. I spent eleven months on the wait list for that doctor; there just wasn't enough

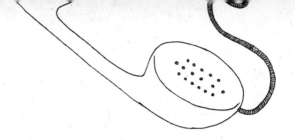

care available for the number of patients in the system. That waiting period was extremely difficult for me, because I had no way of knowing when it would end. They didn't tell me that I had eleven months to wait. Instead I was in limbo, waiting by the door every day for my letter, watching my twentieth birthday pass by while the face of a thirteen-year-old boy was reflected back at me in the hall mirror.

The long wait for trans patients is plain dangerous. Trans people can experience huge emotional distress because of their body dysphoria, and if they don't receive treatment, the results can be deadly.

The suicide rate among trans people is huge—in America, 40 percent of them have attempted suicide at some point.

It's heartbreaking and truly scary to think about how many lives might have been lost because a trans person felt helpless, waiting for a letter that never seemed to arrive.

I still remember the day I got my doctor's letter. After eleven months, you start to feel that it's never going to happen, so when I received a picture of an unexpected letter from my mum on WhatsApp, I was stunned. I couldn't concentrate at college for the rest of the day, and the bus journey home was agonizingly slow. It was all kind of a blur until I finally held the letter in my hands and read the appointment date out loud. It was just four weeks away.

Thankfully, I was incredibly lucky to be put under the care of a doctor at the clinic who understood the frustration of waiting so long. At that first appointment, he quickly gave the go-ahead for hormones, set in motion the blood tests, and sent a detailed letter to my general practioner about all the future care that would be needed. I'm really grateful for that, but if I had known that I was so close to hormones when I was waiting endlessly for my first doctor's appointment, I would probably have felt a lot more positive. Even if nothing can be done about the wait, something must be done about the communication between clinics and patients.

To be put on testosterone, I needed to get a fasting blood test to check out various health indicators, such as my liver function, and to get a baseline reading of my hormone levels so they would know how to adjust my doses in the future. I'd never had a blood test before, so going in was pretty nerve-racking. Luckily, my mum refused to let me go in alone. I sat in a small room with her and a nice yet straight-to-the-point nurse named Mary, who looked at my file and examined the list of samples I needed to provide. She told us that the system said I needed to give a semen sample, which made us laugh hysterically. I responded, "That could be a problem!"

Boom. A sudden wave of nausea hit, making my stomach churn.

The actual blood test was fine—that is, up until the third vial, when I realized I could hear my blood trickling into the tube and started to feel a little weird. During the fourth vial, I felt my arm going cold and wondered why. I felt a cotton swab on my arm, noticed Mary and my mum staring at me, heard them speaking faster and faster, and then my vision went hazy. I don't know what happened after that. I opened my eyes to see my mum holding my head down between my legs and the nurse running out of the room, only to come back holding candy. My mum told me I had fainted, and all I managed to slur out in response was "Well, am I okay?"

Boom. A sudden wave of nausea hit, making my stomach churn. Thankfully, it didn't last long. After a couple pieces of candy, I was up and out of there, ready to start testosterone.

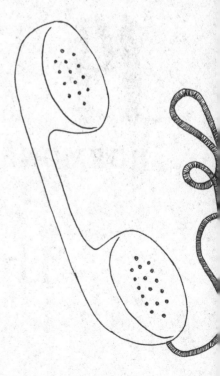

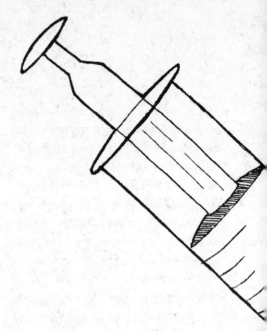

14

HORMONE TREATMENT

The quest to
a beard!

By the next month, I was lying on a chair with a syringeful of testosterone in my butt cheek. I felt a little exposed, with a growing pain around the injection site that felt almost like a huge bruise, but I was also really relieved to finally be starting my physical transition into manhood. I had expected to be so excited that I'd run out of the surgery screaming with joy, but instead I limped back to the car like an old man, groaning about the pain in my butt!

I get an injection roughly every twelve weeks to keep my testosterone levels within the correct range and will have to for the rest of my life if I want to keep the wonderful changes the hormone treatment has brought about. On top of that, I have regular blood tests to monitor my liver and cholesterol, psychotherapy appointments to check my mental health, and specialist doctor appointments to make sure I'm physically in shape. It sounds like a lot, but if that's what it takes to live a happy life, I'll do it.

This medical journey is by no means an easy process. Not all professionals know how to treat trans patients: I had countless hold-ups due to doctors not understanding where I needed to be referred to or canceled appointments that made time-sensitive injections a nightmare.

It's so important to keep on top of all the appointments. Missing them can lead to your treatment being taken away, and being late for your injections can screw up your hormone levels.

Testosterone, also known as T, comes in different forms: injections, patches, and gels. At my gender identity clinic, they offered me the choice between injections or gel. There are pros and cons to each, so it's best to pick the one that most suits your lifestyle. The choice doesn't stop there: there are different types of injections, patches, and gels, so do your research thoroughly. Pills used to be available too, but they've been banned in many countries because of the negative effects they've been found to have on the liver.

I decided to go for injections of a slow-release T called Nebido, administered by a nurse about every three months. There is testosterone available

This
medical
journey
is by
no means
an easy
process.

that can be self-injected weekly, but I don't think I could've kept up with such frequent treatment because of my work schedule, and besides—the thought of having to regularly self-inject freaks me out! I'd be terrified of doing it wrong. The frequent injections can also make your testosterone levels spike and fluctuate rapidly, whereas Nebido slowly builds up, then very slowly tapers off. I considered gels, but you have to apply them to the same patch of skin at the same time every day after showering, and you can't let them come into contact with anyone else. A few too many rules for me! Having said that, I'd prefer gel over weekly injections, and they'd be great for anyone needle-phobic. It's all about personal preference.

My testosterone is a thick, oily liquid that is slowly administered via deep intramuscular injection, a.k.a. my butt. There's a lot of liquid, which means it's not exactly a standard pinprick kind of injection. It hurts for the full

TURNS out i fainted and FACEPLANTED. OUCH.

length of the injection, which can take from as little as twenty seconds to as long as two minutes.

Personally I don't mind the pain, but that's coming from someone who loves getting tattoos and has a pretty high pain tolerance.

Usually I'm given the choice of lying down or standing up when I get the injection, because lying down can help your muscles relax, making the shot faster and less painful. But for my most recent injection, I had a different nurse who seemed to be in a hurry. I stood up for the first time to keep everything as quick as possible—bad idea. It was really painful, and after she'd finished, I went to leave, blinked, and found myself on the floor with a huge pain across my chest. Turns out I fainted and faceplanted. Ouch.

Assuming you don't manage injure yourself, an ache normally hangs around for three or four days after a T shot, so I wouldn't recommend throwing yourself around. Some people say the ache goes away more quickly if you exercise or apply a small amount of heat, but I just take it easy and wait for it to go away on its own. It might sound off-putting, but that small amount of pain is such a tiny price to pay for a treatment that is so life-changing.

Besides, transitioning is never going to be easy. If you decide to medically transition, you need to be ready to commit to a lifetime of treatment. There are regular blood tests, hormones, psychotherapy, check-ups—not to mention any surgery you might feel you need. You also have to think about your life in the long term.

It can be difficult for young trans people to think seriously about whether they might want to have children when getting hormones as quickly as possible is at the forefront of their minds.

But fertility and family planning are really important considerations. At the moment, doctors don't really know what the long-term effects of testosterone might be on egg production. So before I was prescribed T, my doctor asked if I wanted to get my eggs cryopreserved for the future. For a nineteen-year-old, it was a pretty heavy question, considering my mum still made me dinner and washed my clothes. I decided not to opt for any fertility treatment; I want to adopt in the future, but I've never had a desire to have my own children.

As much as I love what social media has done for bringing the trans community closer together, it's added a lot of expectation. Some guys make videos of their changes and sometimes, within just a few months of being on testosterone, they have full beards, muscles, the works! Even I was a sucker for those expectations at first, but changes happen differently for each person. The internet can be kind of a crappy place when it shoves a bunch of sad trans people together. If you're a part of online communities and you're finding yourself getting sad or jealous, take a step back.

There are different ways to combat dysphoria, and my approach is a combination of hormone treatment and, most importantly, willpower. Many trans people see the general goal of their transition as hormones. But trust me, your problems don't go away after your first dose.

It's a very slow process and not everyone is guaranteed the same results.

For trans men, T treatment may bring changes such as increased body and facial hair, a breaking voice, thinning hair, fat redistribution, muscle/weight gain, and more. It sounds great, but not everyone has the same experience on testosterone. Some guys will get a beard after four months, whereas others don't have one chin hair after six years.

Willpower is my number one way to fight dysphoria.

The day I got my first T shot was kind of anticlimactic. It was like a birthday—you wait for ages for it to come, get all excited, and when it finally arrives…it's just another day. I didn't feel dramatically different the second testosterone was in my system.

I confidently say that willpower is my number one way to fight dysphoria. Solutions don't just appear before you—you have to work for them. For example, if your chest is bothering you, use your willpower until you manage to get a binder; if you're scared to use men's restrooms, take a friend or use a stand-to-pee device. The best thing about willpower is that, if you have it, you're guaranteed to be able to help yourself. For example, when I was younger I was terrified to use the men's restrooms. One day while exploring a cathedral (of all places!), I decided to take the plunge when nobody was around and use their men's room. I came out and held up my arms in victory to the sound of my friend cheering.

For a while, willpower worked really well. Whenever I was feeling dysphoric, I'd somehow find a way to take another small step in my transition, which gave me a nice little boost. However, there's only so much you can do by yourself, and my resources started running a little dry toward the end of my wait for testosterone. I noticed myself falling back into little pits of dysphoria once in a while, which is when I realized I needed to keep busy. Being at college and having coursework to do really helped ease my dysphoria because there was always a looming deadline that could capture my attention instead of my negative thoughts. I ended up with top grades after my four years in higher education, so you can tell how much time I put into it.

There were times when getting on T felt impossible, but despite the minefields within trans health care, I finally got there. Some guys report an increase in temper on testosterone, but emotionally I haven't changed. My personality is still the same, although I'm a lot more positive and forward-thinking now.

It's really satisfying knowing that the correct hormone is in my body and I'm not on a wait list with no end in sight.

I'm fortunate in that my changes on testosterone have definitely met my expectations. I was most excited for my voice to drop quickly, because it was making me seem way younger than I actually was.

Before hormones, people always used to compliment my more neutral-sounding voice, but looking back, I think I sounded like a chipmunk. My voice was so soft! That's the beauty of my videos—I love being able to look back and actually see the difference to how I am now. They especially helped at first—I didn't realize certain changes were happening until I looked back at a video from a month before. I had to get through a phase of not being able to control my voice cracking and squeaking for a while. Just so embarrassing!

At one point, I was scared to talk because I didn't know what was going to come out of my mouth.

Thankfully, within three months my voice had deepened considerably, and continued to do so until I'd been on testosterone for about six months. The voice drop is definitely the thing people notice first if they haven't seen me in a while. When I say my first word, they're surprised by how deep it is!

The next thing on my wish list was for my menstrual cycle to stop. This was a bit of a gamble—whether a cycle completely stops on testosterone varies from person to person. Thankfully, after two months mine stopped completely and never came back. If you're on testosterone and still struggling with this, make sure your T levels are high enough, just in case that

I THINK i sounded like A CHIPMUNK.

might help. If they're too low, your cycle isn't likely to stop.

Something nobody told me about and that caught me off guard was the "chubby phase."

Between four and six months on testosterone, I noticed that my cheeks looked chubby and that I had gained weight. The weight must have redistributed somewhere else, because the chubbiness in my face has gone, but the extra weight remains. I used to be a measly 99 pounds, but about ten months later I've crept up to 119 pounds. Something else that caught me off guard was my body odor. Pretty much every bodily fluid smells different after testosterone. It sounds gross, but it's not really as bad as it seems—just different and strong. I find that the smells are most intense right after my T shot.

A really desirable change for me was, of course, facial hair. The quest to a beard! Beard growth depends on a number of factors, and there's no guarantee that you'll be blessed by the hair gods. Some guys go years on testosterone with only patchy sprouts of hair to show for it. With that in mind, after around seven months on T, I began using Minoxidil, which is a hair growth treatment for scalp hair loss and balding. It's not supposed to be used on your face, but many guys, both cis and trans, use it to accelerate beard growth with great results. I decided to try it out of pure curiosity. After one month of use, I noticed a bunch of hair under my chin; after two months, I had a face full of darker hairs. I can't credit the growth solely to Minox because I'm on testosterone too, but wow! Whatever I did worked, so I'm not complaining.

These days, fifteen months after starting hormones, I can grow a pretty good amount of hair across my face, although I'm still waiting for my beard and tiny mustache to connect.

The change that gets most glossed over in the lead-up to hormone therapy is the enlargement of the clitoris (which from now on I will call "T-dick," because using female terms for my genitals makes me feel uncomfortable). It's an extremely common change that often happens very early on. I noticed things getting bigger after just two weeks on T, which was insane—nobody had told me that it'd be the first thing I'd notice. If you're looking to start T, I'd really recommend not wearing tight underwear for a while—things get sensitive. You can thank me later! Growth is a really important goal for a lot of trans guys, because the T-dick can resemble a very small penis if you're lucky. There are also aids such as pumps and special creams available to help you

Some people have to wait years after starting hormones before seeing any change.

promote growth too, each with pros and cons.

On testosterone, your body shape changes due to fat redistribution and muscle gain. I have a very thin body type. That hasn't changed on T, but after four months I noticed my shoulders start to get broader and my chest appear to get flatter. Fat redistribution doesn't necessarily happen right away though. Some people have to wait years after starting hormones before seeing any change. Muscle gain was also one of those false promises I'd heard on the internet, so let me set the record straight: if you want muscles, you have to work for them. Testosterone won't magically turn you into Terminator Arnold Schwarzenegger.

There are three Hs that famously tend to appear alongside testosterone treatment: horny, hot, and hungry. Hunger wasn't an issue for me. I had the odd hot flush during the first week on T, but after that I don't remember feeling my

body heat change. As for my libido, it definitely peaked for a few months but has calmed down dramatically since. It's hard to say whether that was brought on by the hormone itself—I think a lot of it was down to finally feeling confident enough in my body to want to have sex, even if the physical changes weren't immediate.

Personally, I think one of the three Hs should be changed to "hairy," because Jeeeeeesus do you get hairy on testosterone—and I don't just mean on your face!

I never had much of a happy trail before T, but these days I'm sporting quite a nice rug on my stomach—not to mention my legs. Before T, I had really hairy legs, but only from the knee down, like weird bristly leg warmers. Nowadays I'm practically Bigfoot everywhere below the waist. And I really do mean *everywhere*.

15

TOP SURGERY

He asked
me to take
my shirt off.

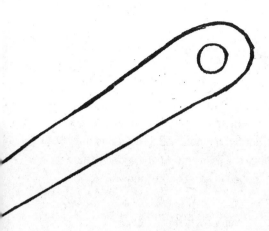

Not all trans guys get surgery to remove breast tissue, but for a lot of us, top surgery is an essential part of transitioning. When I looked in the mirror, my chest was my main focus of dysphoria and it stopped me from doing things other guys could do without even thinking, like going to a pool or taking my shirt off at the beach. It even affected me physically—since you're advised to avoid doing heavy exercise in a chest binder, I couldn't work out at the gym or go for a run.

Luckily, there are surgeons out there who specialize in chest reconstruction for trans guys, and who achieve some spectacular (I'm resisting the urge to type "pectacular") results. There are all kinds of different top surgeries, but I wanted to give the lowdown on two very popular types: **double incision (DI)** and **peri-areolar (peri)**.

From the diagrams on page 179, you can see the incision lines made during each surgery. In DI, two large incisions go under each pectoral to remove tissue and a smaller one goes around each nipple. The nipples are removed before being cut to size and placed in the correct position. In peri, two circular incisions are made, one around the nipple and a larger one outside the areola. Once the tissue has been removed, the outer circle is pulled in to meet the inner circle.

Both methods have their pros and cons. Peri leaves the least scarring, but most surgeons will only perform the technique on anyone with smaller chests—it doesn't work if there's too much excess skin. Nipple placement with peri is more limited, since the surgeon isn't removing the nipple and replacing it perfectly, but instead leaving it attached. That means that peri results are really varied, whereas DI results are extremely consistent. That being said, DI does leave large scars under the pectorals that will stretch if not well looked after in the early days of recovery—but if taken care of correctly, they will fade very well.

I was hoping to go for peri because my chest was pretty small and I wanted to minimize the amount of scarring, but only my surgeon could tell me what was best.

Months before my surgery, I took a train to my gender identity clinic to meet the man himself, Mr. Andrew Yelland. He was extremely respectful of my body while asking me to take off my shirt and

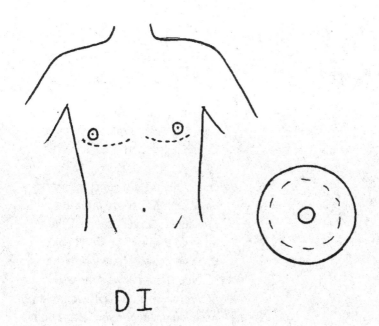

DI

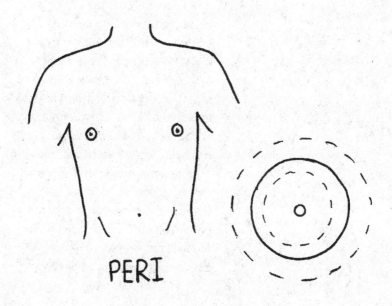

PERI

I was a perfect candidate.

examining my chest. Like music to my ears, Mr. Yelland said I was a perfect candidate for peri-areolar!

One of my biggest concerns was having leftover tissue after the procedure. Surgery seemed like a lot to go through if I wasn't going to be completely happy with the results. There's always the option of a revision, but I really wanted to have it done in one operation. Some people say their biggest fear is losing a nipple, since after the incisions and the general invasiveness of surgery, it can definitely happen. Being a big fan of tattoos and knowing an amazing artist, this didn't worry me at all—there's always a nipple tattoo! Speaking of nipples, losing sensation was also a concern because numbness is extremely common after any surgery, due to nerves getting damaged. It sounds serious, but sensation can return after surgery if nerves reconnect. It's more common to retain nipple sensation with the peri-areolar technique than double incision, because your nipples don't have to be removed completely.

FINE POIN

I was also worried about actually going in for surgery. I'd never been under anesthetic or really hardcore painkillers, so the thought of being so drowsy scared me a lot. I was anxious about the whole hospital experience, to be honest, but once I arrived for my pre-op appointment and met the surgeon, I felt much more at ease. During the appointment, nurses took my blood pressure, did a blood test, measured my height and weight, and did a test for MRSA. I'd heard about the last one and had been dreading it. They needed to swab my nose, which was fine; my armpits, a little weird but still fine; and finally, my groin. Not fine! Or so I thought—in reality it was completely harmless. I just had to lift up both legs of my boxers and they quickly and respectfully swabbed just where my leg connected to my groin. The appointment didn't last very long, but it gave me a chance to familiarize myself with the environment and ask all the stupid questions I wanted.

There's a lot of prep to think about before surgery.

You have to make sure you have everything to take with you to the hospital, rope in people to take care of you post-op, arrange for a safe post-op environment, and, most importantly, stay healthy leading up to the surgery itself. I had surgery in January, right when

I planned everything I could months in advance.

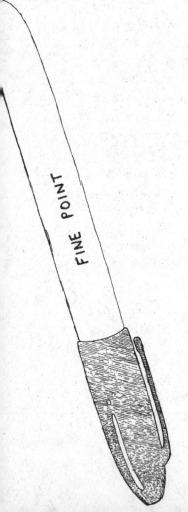

FINE POINT

all the horrible coughs, colds, and flu bugs were flying around everywhere, so I tried to keep myself in a healthy little bubble away from everybody else. I was told to avoid alcohol and cigarettes, and also to take Arnica montana, which reduces bruising and swelling. On top of that, I drank plenty of water, ate plenty of good food, and took vitamin C to boost my immunity. Thankfully, I didn't get sick!

I planned everything I could months in advance. As soon as I found out my surgery date, I asked my parents to come with me for support—and to drive me home. No, really—it was a two-hour drive, and attempting public transport twenty-four hours post-op was not an option! Then all I needed to arrange was getting the time off work, booking a hotel for the night before, and packing everything I needed.

HERE'S MY TOP-SURGERY KIT LIST:

Button-up shirts
Sweatpants
PJ bottoms
Slip-on shoes
Underwear
Anti-itch and allergy pills
Neck pillow
Laxatives
Bed pillow
Wet Wipes
Bathroom stuff
Boyfriend Jake*
Post-op binder
Long phone cord

*Jake was definitely useful in helping me get my underwear on for the first couple of days post-op ...so if you want to retain your dignity, I'd bring somebody you feel really, really comfortable with.

THERE'S always A NiPPLE tattoo!

The most valuable thing to me was probably my long phone cord. I was so restricted in my movement after surgery that stretching my arms out to reach the charger was a big no-no.

I think I would have died of boredom and loneliness without my phone, especially at night.

The other precious item was a pillow from my bed. Honestly, you don't realize how much you move around in a car until you've been cut open and stuck back together again, so having a pillow to cushion my chest against the seat belt was a big relief. Loose-fitting clothes were also really important; since I couldn't lift my arms for about twelve days after surgery, button-up shirts, slip-on shoes, and sweatpants were a must.

The day of surgery came quickly, and before I knew it, I was walking into the Nuffield hospital in Brighton at 7 a.m. with my bag in hand and my family behind me. One of the staff members took us to my room, and my mum immediately started to unpack all my things into every available cupboard and drawer. I think she must have been hiding things on purpose so that I had to get out of bed once I'd had surgery, because I could barely find anything after that.

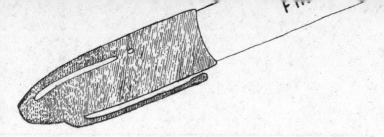

I nervously sat on the edge of the bed until the head nurse, Peter, arrived. He told me I was first on the list to have surgery at 8:30 a.m. and that he needed to take some readings. My heart rate was insanely high and he expressed concern, but I'm pretty sure it was just because nerves were eating me alive. Peter left the room and reappeared shortly after with a hospital gown, compression socks, and some rather handsome cotton underwear.

The next person I saw was my surgeon, the glorious Mr. Yelland. He asked me to sit on the bed and take my shirt off so he could mark up my chest, which was a ridiculous sight.

The man who was going to change my life forever was looming over me, brandishing a Sharpie to draw around my nipples.

After Mr. Yelland left, I put on my hospital garb with a little help from Jake and reluctantly got into the bed. Then everything started happening quickly. I remember being wheeled down the hallway by two members of staff as my family followed behind me. We left them behind once we passed through a set of doors. The moment those doors opened, everything started to look more like a hospital. I was really nervous and tried to keep my eyes focused on what was in front of me rather than the equipment surrounding us. We went through another set of doors into a very small room filled with a few nurses, my surgeon, and the anesthetist.

I'd never had surgery before, and I'd wondered a lot about the next part. What was it like being put under? Would I know it was happening? Would they tell me to count back from ten? The anesthetist and a really friendly nurse chatted with me about what I did for work, all the while fiddling with little bottles and the cannula to put into my hand for the anesthesia and medication. Then all I can remember is one of them saying, "This might feel a little cold," while the other reclined the bed.

I felt a prickly sensation in my throat, and I was out before the bed was flat.

I opened my eyes an hour and a half later and my first thought was *I'm so cold*. My confused brain eventually realized I was in recovery with a mask over my face. There was a nurse beside me, and all I managed to say was "I'm so cold," probably about one hundred times. I looked around the recovery room and noticed the clouds painted on the wall. I can remember thinking how much I wanted to compliment someone—anyone, in fact—about how well the clouds were painted. My memory is pretty fragmented, but I remember being wheeled back to

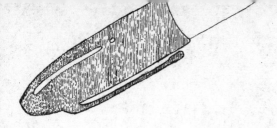

my room and hooked up to tons of machines. It felt like the blood pressure machine went off every two minutes, puffing up the cuff on my arm, waking me up and making a loud beep.

I was dozing for a while, but when I could finally keep myself awake, I realized was in no pain whatsoever. No pain and no nausea . . . a miracle!

I didn't make great company, but my parents and Jake stayed in the room with me for the whole day making small talk. After a while I began to moan, "I'm so hot. Oh my God, I'm sweating," so my mum peeled back the duvet to reveal not one extra blanket, but four. I must have been so cold in recovery! The pain wasn't at all bad, but before long I started to feel extremely achy around my armpits and my ribs. From looking down, I could immediately tell it was because of the compression binder they had put on me after surgery to reduce swelling and fluid build-up. It wasn't like a binder you wear every day; this was a bone-crushing death brace.

Throughout the day, the nurses gave me pain relief such as codeine and paracetamol. It was the longest day ever. I remember repeatedly looking at the clock, chatting away, falling asleep then waking up just thirty minutes later. At 9 p.m. my family left me alone

i grunted like A warthog.

in my room for the night with only a jug of water, a pack of cookies, and a help button.

The next morning was such a relief—I was being discharged at 10 a.m.! I also saw my surgeon for the first time since the surgery. He came in to undo the horrible binder and check on me before I could leave. The noise I made when he ripped that Velcro death trap off was quite frankly inhuman—I grunted like a warthog. But when I looked down, I was completely mind-blown. My chest was so flat! I was still pretty out of it, so all I managed to say to Mr. Yelland was "Thank you so much," over and over. I had a brief chance to breathe before the nurse came in and put me into my own post-op binder I had brought from home. This one gave me a lot more breathing room, but I'd have to keep it on for a week, both day and night, until my post-op appointment. I was allowed two thirty-minute breaks every day, but other than that, it had to stay on.

Before I knew it, I was walking out into the world with my new (fragile!) chest and heading home in the car. Even with my dad's careful driving, every pebble on the road felt like a boulder. But as much discomfort as I was in, I couldn't stop thinking about the fact that my parents were with me. When I came out as transgender at age sixteen, I could never have imagined that I'd have both of my parents showing me such support and compassion throughout my transition.

I couldn't stop thinking about the fact that my parents were with me.

Once I was home and safely deposited on the sofa, it was time to focus on my recovery. Recovery plays a crucial role in determining how your chest will look in the long term, and most surgeons provide aftercare instructions to ensure that the healing process is as smooth and as painless as possible. Pain is something a lot of people worry about when going through top surgery, but honestly, it wasn't that bad! My entire chest was numb, so the only immediate discomfort I felt was rib pain from the hospital binder, and some soreness from swelling on my sides and under my armpits. The rib pain went away after about two days, which was a big relief. The swelling soreness stuck around for a while longer, and once it faded away after two weeks, another kind of discomfort took its place. For the next two weeks, the skin across my chest was sore to the touch, almost like a sunburn. It didn't hurt all the time, just from friction against clothes. I remember this vividly, because I'd gone back to work by

The seven days after surgery are a bit of a blur.

that point and I could not wait to get home for the sweet relief of taking my shirt off.

Getting mobility right during recovery is really important. You need to move, but not too much or too little. Too much too soon and you risk hurting yourself, stretching the scars or messing with the healing process in general. If you move too little, your muscles could seize up, with long-term implications. To keep me going at just the right pace, a physical therapist at the hospital gave me a number of exercises to do with my arms and upper body. It took me a while to pull myself out of the mindset that I was going to hurt myself, but I soon discovered that if I did too much, my body would let me know. When I first came out of surgery, I couldn't raise my arms more than sixty degrees from my sides, but I slowly improved as I did the exercises. I also tried to do as much as possible myself. It's easy to kick back and let everyone do everything for you, because recovery is hard both mentally and physically. I seriously

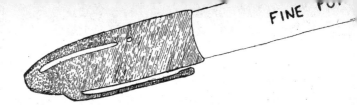

underestimated how tired I would get just walking around the house. But you have to at least try to do things by yourself. I discovered little tricks that made it easier for me to dress myself, make food, and eventually even wash my hair. These things might sound easy, but with really restricted movement they can be a challenge! Don't get me wrong, I had a lot of help when it came to picking up heavy things, getting stuff from shelves, and even closing my pesky bedroom door, but I definitely craved independence. Doing tasks on my own really helped.

The seven days after surgery are a bit of a blur. I just remember waiting for my two binder breaks where I'd be free to look at my flat chest in the mirror, wondering what was underneath all the bandages; my mum and I tried to guess where my nipples were. Before I knew it, it was time to go back to see my surgeon in Brighton to get the staples around my nipples removed. It sounds gross, and trust me, it looked gross too! Thankfully, I was still so numb that I couldn't even feel Mr. Yelland taking them out. I tried not to look at my chest until all the staples were out and he put a mirror in front of me, so when I did, I was completely blown away. Even though my nipples were bloody and unfamiliar, with angry and swollen skin around them, I could already tell my chest was going to turn out perfectly. That wonderful man had performed what felt like a miracle. I don't remember saying much apart from

"Wow," "This is so amazing," and "I can't believe it," but I made sure to shake Mr. Yelland's hand and thank him as sincerely as possible. With teary eyes I told him, "You've changed my life. You really have."

After removing the staples, Mr. Yelland put little pieces of tape over the incisions to keep the skin flat and everything in place. He told me that they would probably fall off when they were ready and that I could shower with them on. Those things ended up causing me a whole world of drama! Roughly a week after the appointment, the tape was still on and wasn't showing any signs of wanting to come off, especially on my right side. My right nipple seemed to be healing more slowly and was bleeding more often. My nips went through a stage of scabbing underneath the tape, which is perfectly normal, but it made getting the tape off really difficult because the scabs came off with it.

I waited as long as I could, taking the strips off one by one, until one day I woke up with what looked like dried blood all around my right nipple.

Panicked, I rushed into the bathroom and decided it was time to take the tape off, since it clearly it wasn't helping anything underneath. When I removed it, I noticed that fluid had been building up, making healing very difficult. For a second, I thought I had an infection, because my incisions were a funny

color, but it turns out that was just because the tissue was "granulating," which is part of the healing process for deep wounds. Luckily my mum knows a lot about wound care, so I texted her some pictures and she told me to clean the area and let it air out. My right nip took a week longer to heal than the other one, but it looks absolutely fine. Nothing to worry about!

Overall, I'm really happy with the results. My nipple placement is great, they're a good size, and things are pretty symmetrical. For a while my left side was more swollen, but it seems to be going down over time. If I had to pick something—and I'm being completely over-critical here—my left nipple is a circle, whereas my right is more of an oval. But it isn't noticeable and it doesn't bother me in the slightest. I'm a very, very happy boy!

All of this amazing medical treatment is lifesaving. I don't think I could have lived in a world where it wasn't available. I couldn't bear to live my life being so unhappy with my body. I'm incredibly fortunate in that my surgery was free and paid for by the UK's health care service, but I'm acutely aware that this isn't the case for most other people around the world. I've heard numbers ranging from $6,000 to $10,000 for top surgery in the United States, which is why you'll find hundreds of fundraisers online from guys looking for help. The next time you're feeling like doing a good deed and have some spare cash lying around, please consider finding one of these fundraisers online and donating. Surgery is an impossible dream for some.

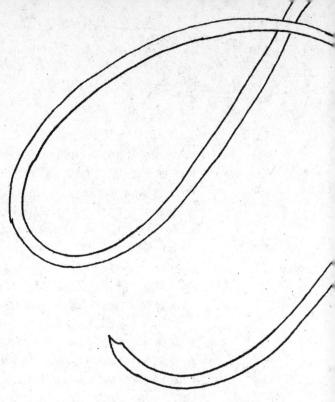

16

BOTTOM SURGERY

I'd much rather wait.

Not all trans people choose to physically transition through hormones and surgeries. It's important to remember that everyone's journey is different and, in the UK at least, you can pick and choose the treatments you need to be happy. For example, I personally don't want to have bottom surgery because I don't feel like the results of the procedures available right now will make me feel 100 percent happy. But I know many trans people who have had bottom surgery and have never looked back.

A lot of people refer to bottom surgery as "the op." But "the op" is a lot less common than they think. Bottom surgery options for trans men are limited and intense. Let me try to explain the basics of two techniques.

Phalloplasty is a very popular option right now. Surgeons seem to perform it in a few different ways, so I'm going to do my best to explain it just how I've come to understand it. Skin is taken from the arm or thigh and used to create a very basic penis with one testicle. It's then sculpted to have a glans, along with a urethral hook-up so you can pee out of it. You can also choose to bury your T-dick (clitoris) at the base of the penis if you want to, so that you can achieve orgasm. Finally, you're given a second testicle containing a pump, which enables erections.

This surgery is very intense in recovery because of all the wounds that need tending to, but at the end of it all you get a great-looking and working penis capable of (but not guaranteed) to achieve penetration, orgasm, and urination.

That might sound like the obvious choice, but a lot of thought needs to go into opting for this procedure. For a start, not all results are the same and there can be all sorts of complications with sensation, urination, and the use of the erectile device later on. It's currently pretty rare to undergo the many stages of phallo without having any complications.

Metoidioplasty is something I hadn't heard of until recently, and yes, it's a big word. Again, I won't be able to do this surgery justice from my basic explanation, but it's pretty amazing. The operation is a lot shorter than with phalloplasty, and it uses the already existing growth of your T-dick. The surgeon cuts the skin under your T-dick so that when erect, it stands up and may be able to be used for penetration.

At this stage in my life, I have very little desire to undergo either of these procedures.

That can be it, or you can also have more done. The surgeon can lengthen your urethra and make it go through and out your T-dick so you can pee through it. Then if you choose, they can use more existing skin to house testicular implants. This surgery can be done alongside a hysterectomy and vaginectomy so that your old organs are removed and everything else is buried under your new equipment. Woo! However, again, "perfect" results are not guaranteed. As with all surgeries, anything can happen when your surgeon actually gets to work, let alone when the healing process starts to begin.

At this stage in my life, I have very little desire to undergo either of these procedures. Phalloplasty is probably the technique I'd prefer in terms of looks and function, but the recovery is extremely intense and the skin graft from the arm or thigh leaves huge scarring, which definitely doesn't appeal to me. Metoidioplasty is attractive because huge grafts aren't needed, but I wouldn't be happy with the size of the phallus. I do have

There's
more to
BEING
transgender
THAN feeling
uncomfortable
ABOUT your
GENITALIA.

bottom dysphoria, but I'd much rather wait to see how these techniques progress and keep everything I have intact, ready for when a surgery I really want becomes available.

I'd like to address a few bottom surgery myths, because I think there's a lot of confusion and miseducation out there.

1. All trans guys should want bottom surgery.
There's more to being transgender than feeling uncomfortable about your genitalia. As I've tried to explain, not everyone feels dysphoria in the same ways. Some people may choose not to have bottom surgery because they're okay with what they have in their pants, and other people might just decide they don't like the techniques available to them.

2. Bottom surgery is purely cosmetic.
This could be said of any surgery relating to gender identity, and it's given as an excuse for not providing health insurance or health care services to fund these surgeries. It's the most infuriating sentence I hear come out of someone's mouth. For a lot of people, these surgeries are the difference between life and death. Some people see their bodies as prisons, stopping them from living an ordinary life. Without our free UK health care service, I wouldn't have had access to treatment for a long time, which would have seriously damaged my mental health.

Treatment for trans people is no different than the treatment you receive when you're in any other form of pain or suffering: it's essential.

3. Trans surgeries mutilate the body.
The definition of "mutilate" is to damage or dismember a part of the body by removal or destruction. As a trans man, I feel there is something wrong with my body—it doesn't match up to the gender inside my head. By having surgery, I'm repairing my body, not mutilating it.

4. Bottom surgery doesn't look realistic.
People come in all different shapes and sizes, and each cisgender man's penis looks different. Different doesn't mean unrealistic. Someone's just had surgery to construct a penis—how much more real does it get?!

5. Bottom surgery is too risky.
Every kind of surgery has risks. Hell, even getting a tooth pulled has risks in the fine print that nobody bothers to read. Not as many people have bottom surgery as have their teeth pulled, so the procedures evolve at a slower pace. But they're progressing faster than you might think, with more and more people getting fantastic results. Besides, for a lot of people, the benefit and improvement to their lives far outweighs the risk.

Bottom surgery definitely isn't for everyone, but there's nothing wrong with the results you can achieve with the techniques available. If you're not 100 percent sure, don't rush into anything. Look online at forums or blogs to check out pictures of results and ask questions.

The trans community is ridiculously open—I'm sure there's someone out there who can give you some advice!

While I've spent the last few chapters discussing medical routes to transition, there's also what is known as "natural transition." This is when someone chooses not to undergo hormone therapy or surgery, and instead opts for other methods like dieting, supplements, and weight training to alter their body. Whichever path someone chooses to take, it doesn't make them any more or less trans. There's a lot of pressure to sign up for hormones and surgery as quickly as possible, but it might not be for everyone.

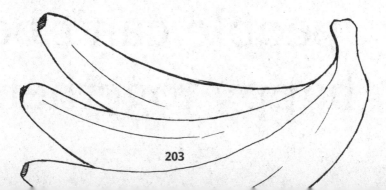

17

DATING AS TRANS

Don't let anyone tell you two trans people can't be happy together.

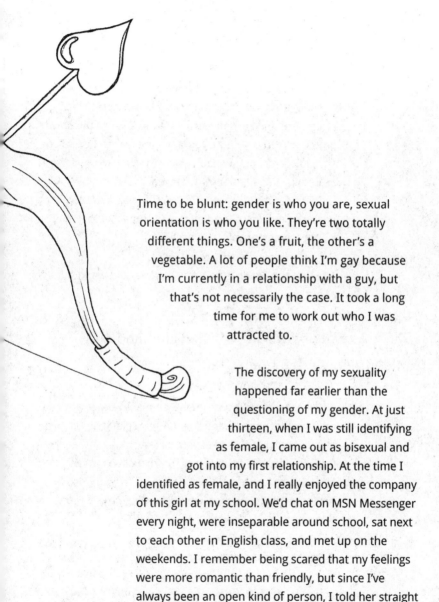

Time to be blunt: gender is who you are, sexual orientation is who you like. They're two totally different things. One's a fruit, the other's a vegetable. A lot of people think I'm gay because I'm currently in a relationship with a guy, but that's not necessarily the case. It took a long time for me to work out who I was attracted to.

The discovery of my sexuality happened far earlier than the questioning of my gender. At just thirteen, when I was still identifying as female, I came out as bisexual and got into my first relationship. At the time I identified as female, and I really enjoyed the company of this girl at my school. We'd chat on MSN Messenger every night, were inseparable around school, sat next to each other in English class, and met up on the weekends. I remember being scared that my feelings were more romantic than friendly, but since I've always been an open kind of person, I told her straight up. To my surprise, she told me she felt the same way, which was amazing. Unfortunately, we were then stuck, out of contact with each other because I was going on a school trip to Paris. With my mind elsewhere, it was really hard to take in the sights. To this day, it's the only time I've been out of the country. I really wish I could go abroad again, but I just don't have the time to organize everything I need to apply for a new passport now that my name and gender marker has changed. That and because I'm kind of terrified that in some places they still treat trans people like criminals.

Anyway, the whole time I was in Paris, all I could think about was this girl.

Hell, I was walking through Disneyland and all I wanted to do was go home!

This was tough, because that relationship ended after only about a year. But during the course of it, I switched from identifying as a bisexual to a lesbian. Back then, I think I had a very narrow view on sexuality and felt I needed to just hurry up and decide. So, with me having virtually no experience of dating boys, I ruled them out.

During the next couple of years I went through a few failed relationships (if you can call them that when you're thirteen to fifteen!), before eventually I started

I started developing a crush on one of my best male friends.

developing a crush on one of my best male friends. It really confused me because I was 100 percent sure that I liked girls and girls only. When I told my friend, I tried hard to be as honest as possible, saying that I really wasn't sure what I was feeling, but that I'd like to give it a try if he felt something too. He's a really mature and intelligent guy, so after saying he felt the same way, he agreed to see where it went.

We tried things out for a week, but I quickly found I just couldn't do it. At the time I didn't understand why, so I blamed it on the fact that he was a boy, but now I realize all the attraction was there: he looked great, had an awesome personality, and our interests were almost identical. But at the end of the day, I was jealous. I wanted to be him. I was so envious of his body that it ended up ruining any chance of a relationship. After that, we drifted apart and didn't speak for years, but recently we met up for his first pride parade. It was amazing to reconnect!

i saw being STRAIGHT as THiS LAST thread of "NORMALITY" that i had TO HOLD on TO.

My next relationship began after I started identifying as male when I was sixteen. My transliness did have an impact on my sexuality. When I still identified as female, I said I was attracted to women, making me a lesbian. However, when I realized my true gender identity was male, liking women actually made me straight.

So, not long after I came out as trans, I started dating someone who at first identified as female, but then came out as a trans a few months into our relationship. This was a massive eye-opener for me:

I went into the relationship with a girlfriend, but then had to start telling people I had a boyfriend.

His coming out wasn't a big deal to me because as a person he didn't change, and after all, I was trans too. The only issue I had was that it made me more confused than ever about my sexuality. I thought I was only attracted to girls, but there I was, in love with a man.

For a while, I started defending my rigid straight identity, saying that my boyfriend was my "exception"—which was wrong on so many levels. I think I did it because I saw being straight as this last thread of "normality" that I had to hold on to. Eventually, being with him made me realize that yes, I was attracted to men too.

That yearlong relationship broke down so many of the barriers I had put up since coming out.

But unfortunately it ended, and again it was because of my jealousy. He was getting further in his transition than I was, and he had the most amazing support from his family. Seeing him get everything I desperately wanted just broke me.

Jealousy is a huge issue when it comes to transitioning. I mentioned before that I steered clear of watching trans people online when I was struggling. The same thing happened in my relationships, both romantic and friendly. Seeing trans people progress made me collapse, so I avoided getting close to them. It got to the point where I'd far prefer to spend time with someone who wasn't trans, because I didn't have to think about their progressing transition.

My jealousy and self-hatred were big factors in why it took about two years for me to want to get involved in another relationship. There was one girl at college I got along with really well; we'd laugh and flirt. But when it came down to her wanting to be close to me, I couldn't stand it—it made my skin crawl. It wasn't her, I just think I had so much self-hatred that the very thought of someone touching

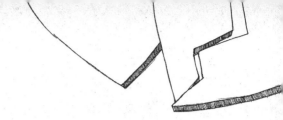

my body made me disgusted. She had no idea I was trans, and I didn't feel ready to out myself to her. I couldn't explain my behavior without coming out, so instead I told her that my life was complicated and I couldn't think about commitments. We haven't spoken since.

As it turned out, I started dating the guy I've been with for the last three years not long after I turned her down. Couldn't think about commitments? Um . . .

My boyfriend's name is Jake, and we got together in spring 2014. He's also a transgender man, and I don't think I could have opened up to him so quickly if he wasn't. There's just something so easy about being with someone you don't have to explain yourself to. Sometimes, when dysphoria hits, you have to sleep with your shirt on or get changed in the other room. We both just get it.

I never really thought about how other people viewed my relationships until I started dating Jake. When we first got together we were in that honeymoon phase, holding hands everywhere. Then one day at a bus stop someone yelled homophobic abuse out of their parked car. That's when I realized, *Oh fuck. This is pretty gay!*

Jake (stupidly) put his middle finger up and the guy in the car tried to scare us by opening the door and pretending to get out. It was terrifying.

That isn't the only time we've faced aggressive homophobia, and since then we've avoided PDA out of pure fear.

When I was younger and in "lesbian relationships," people were never aggressive, but for some reason when seeing a gay male couple, they resort to violence and verbal abuse.

Jake is the reason I found the strength to begin my physical transition. He was already in the public health care system and knew how to work through it, so he offered his help when I was feeling very alone, desperately waiting for my parents to understand. Transitioning didn't affect our relationship until we were both getting treatment. We'd considered the impact it might have and thought we knew what to expect, but we really had no idea. The first hurdle came when we both got letters to see a psychotherapist at the gender identity clinic at the same time. We had both been assigned the same lady and didn't think anything of it—until the day of my appointment, when she told me it was against their policies to have two patients in a relationship seeing the same therapist. Jake was the one who

Jake is the REASON i found the strength.

had his appointment pushed back by two weeks so another psychotherapist could be found.

Fast-forward a year later and that's when the issues really started. We were both roughly at the same stage of transition, both waiting and hoping desperately for our doctor appointments. The months passed, and I got my first appointment.

I went along, heard the amazing news about my testosterone treatment starting soon . . . and Jake was still on the damn wait list. I can't imagine how he must have felt.

Jake told me he didn't want to hear anything about my transition unless it was "new information." I understood why—I could see he was devastated. But I had been waiting for testosterone for so long, and all I wanted to do was celebrate. It was a huge moment in my life and was only going to happen once, so being turned away by him was really hard.

Frustration, sadness, and petty arguments followed on both sides for the next two or three months. I'm not going to lie, there were moments when I didn't know whether we were going to come out of it together. But the week before my first T shot, Jake received his doctor's appointment date. It very nearly brought him to tears with happiness. On the train home from the clinic, we stared at each other in disbelief, only able to occasionally utter "Holy shit!" and "Oh my God."

Our relationship changed again after I had my top surgery.

Since then, I've rarely seen Jake with his shirt off. Before the surgery it was easier, because we were both in the same boat. Now it's hard on both sides: he feels more self-conscious, and I don't want to rub it in his face; I'm not shirtless around him often either. It's a little weird—it feels like we've taken a few steps back in our relationship, feeling less comfortable being around each other. I think it's all right though; a drastic change like a new chest is going to take some getting used to.

Despite that bump in the road, these days our relationship is the best it's ever been. Don't let anyone tell you two trans people can't be happy together. It's like going through puberty, but you're doing it with someone you love, seeing each other change and being aware of each other's needs. We go to almost every one of each other's appointments for support—sometimes they dig up emotions that are hard to deal with alone. The train home from the clinic has seen some tears, for sure!

These days, I believe that sexuality is fluid and that I'm going to like who I like.

These days, I believe that sexuality is fluid and that I'm going to like who I like, regardless of their gender. The word for this is "pansexual." It allows me to say, "Hey, I don't care if you're a guy, girl, both, neither, or whatever—if I like you, I like you."

Sometimes I think about what life would be like if I were a single trans man navigating the world of dating. I wonder how I'd even go about finding someone I could trust or who would love me for who I am. I have no idea how a gay man or straight woman would react to my body. They're attracted to men, and I check all the boxes—except the one labeled "Has a penis." I don't think I'd be outraged if someone rejected me because of that—you can't help what you like (or dislike!). But there's no avoiding the fact that I'd be a little hurt they hadn't even given me a chance.

If I were single, I wouldn't want to limit myself to exclusively dating trans people. But perhaps I'd have to stay within LGBTQ+ circles that have some knowledge of trans issues? I don't know!

I guess it depends on whether I met the person while I was actively searching for a relationship or if we just kind of fell together after having some sort of connection. It would be a lot of work to try to educate each new prospect on every single first date, whereas if I were to meet someone in the real world, we'd get to know each other more naturally.

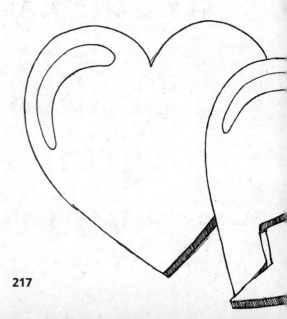

18

SEX & INTIMACY

Sex can be great, even if you're trans!

Before and during coming out, I had difficulties sustaining relationships—although granted, I was still a teenager, so I was hardly the only one! But in particular, I found it incredibly hard to make things work when the other person initiated intimate contact. I'm not even talking about anything sexual—even just cuddling would make me feel insecure because I was so ashamed of my body.

The problem with dysphoria is that it's a negative feeling toward the way your body looks, meaning that some people might have it so bad that sex isn't even an option. Since coming out as trans, I've only ever been in relationships with other trans men, so I can't say for sure if I'd find it easy to engage in sexual activity with a cisgender person. I'm definitely attracted to cisgender people, but I wouldn't want to look at a cis man and feel jealous, or look at a cis woman and feel really uncomfortable.

When you're getting down to business with a trans person, it's important to know what not to say. Using the wrong term for a part of their body can completely kill the mood, but it's not like there are universally used alternatives for different parts. Instead, you just have to make up a dictionary of words to use in place of other words with each new person you want to do stuff with.

For example, some guys will use any variation of "penis" in place of the word "clitoris," because it's easier on dysphoria to use a male term.

It's all down to personal preference and how comfortable you are with your body.

Getting intimate is always going to be an issue when you're uncomfortable with your body, but the decision about whether to keep a binder on or take it off is pretty specific to trans men. It totally depends on what you feel happy with; I felt closer to somebody when my binder was off, but then the lights needed to be off completely for me to feel comfortable. I couldn't stand me or anyone else getting a glimpse of my bare chest. But taking a binder off can be tricky, so it's not always the most attractive moment in the bedroom—you just have to own it! You eventually learn your own way of getting it on and off quickly, and there's nothing wrong with a little binder trouble making you both giggle.

A lot of people think it's perfectly okay to ask what's in my pants and how I have sex. I understand that it's difficult to find out information about trans people's genitals online, but it's a really intrusive question and unless you know me really well, you shouldn't be asking. But for the sake of this book, the short answer is this: everyone is different. Not all transgender guys have the same "equipment," because some have had surgery and some haven't. Even for those who have had an operation, there are so many different kinds of surgeries that there isn't even one straight answer.

I've thought a lot about relationships between gay cis men and trans men. If I were single right now, I don't know how I'd go about pursuing a relationship with a cisgender man. My immediate thought is that it would be easiest to find a guy who identifies as bisexual, because it wouldn't matter whether I'd had bottom surgery or not.

A lot of people think it's perfectly okay to ask what's in my pants and how I have sex.

it's SO important to be SAFE.

My fear with approaching gay men is that they might not want to be with me if I haven't had bottom surgery. And yet, when I've spoken with gay male friends, some of them have said it wouldn't bother them at all. To be honest, I doubt this would ever be a problem. If I'm interested in someone, I'm completely upfront with them about being trans.

That brings me to another important topic: disclosure.

In my opinion, if you're going to sleep with someone, they need to know you're trans before you've even agreed to do the deed.

I'm saying this to anyone pre-op, because it's so important to be safe. I've heard stories of people finding out and turning violent because they're either against trans people or it's just not what they're looking for. I don't think it's always necessary to disclose once you've had both top and bottom surgery, because by that stage it's not really relevant. But some argue that you should always be frank about it, so if you feel like you should, you should. If I was completely post-op and someone still turned me down because of the way my body used to be, I wouldn't want to be with them anyway.

As for how trans men have sex, that also varies from person to person. What I can tell you is that we make it work.

So, on to the not-so-PG-13 part of the book:

There are all kinds of things out there to aid a trans man's "adventures," so let's start with packers. Packers come in different types for different uses. First, there are "soft packers." These are used to create a bulge in your underwear and can range from prosthetic penises with different levels of realism to just some socks safety-pinned to your underwear. Most realistic packers come with a harness under your underwear to hold it in place, but sometimes they wriggle their way out of there. One of the first times I tried packing, I had a poorly made DIY harness and my packer somehow found a way to spin around about one hundred times as I was walking around, slowly making its way out of my underwear.

I can confirm that there's nothing scarier than the fear of a squishy penis falling down your pant leg in the middle of a supermarket.

Personally I've always found soft packers to be kind of a menace, because I can never seem to get a prosthetic that's an appropriate size and fits right in my underwear without creating a bulge that's just way too big. In terms of comfort, socks are my preferred choice, but they obviously lack a certain realism and are just ridiculous. One time, my boyfriend was packing with socks but gave up on them halfway through the day. Seeing him pull a bundled pair of socks out of his pants and straight into a park trash can, while breathing a sigh of relief, almost made me piss myself laughing.

Next, there are "hard packers," and as the name suggests, they're hard . . . and used for sex.

Again, these can come in all different shapes and sizes and are worn with a harness. Harnesses can be more comfy than they sound and range from lightweight jockstraps to boxers with a little pouch. My first experience hard-packing was really weird. It was like reliving my first time. It's a completely different way of doing things! Having tried them out, I'm not a fan of wearing hard packers, because they don't feel enough like my own equipment. Harnesses can be quite clumsy and don't look very natural, and the actual packers that go with them are often expensive or, again, really unrealistic.

Then you have "stand-to-pee" or STP devices, which are used to stand to pee. Some double as packers that you can wear all the time, and others are as basic as a little funnel with a tube. I have an STP that is a three-in-one—you can pack, pee, and play—which is perfect for trans guys with bottom dysphoria, because you can use it for everything a penis does. Having said that, using an STP device is an art and really does take practice. You're essentially peeing horizontally into a small funnel and down a tube, so a common issue with STPs is that you get "backflow," which is exactly what it sounds like—if you bend the STP too much, it can restrict the amount of pee that exits the shaft, meaning it just backs up until you're left with a mess. Trust me, try peeing in a shower or bathtub first to avoid any accidents.

Sexual health is really important in general, but it's even more important for trans people.

It's easy to just ignore your genitals because of dysphoria, but doing so can cause some serious health problems. I know it's not fun to be a man and have to consider pap smears and stuff, but it's necessary.

First up, let's talk about birth control. I've heard trans men say in the past that because they're on testosterone, that means they can't get pregnant. That's definitely not true. If you have not had a hysterectomy, there's always a chance that things could be working at 100 percent efficiency in there,

Let's talk about birth control.

despite your being on T. So, embrace birth control, and talk to a doctor about it.

If you're sexually active, there's always a risk of catching an STI. Testosterone and certain bottom surgeries can actually decrease the amount of natural lubricant you produce, which increases the chances of skin tearing, making it more likely that you could get an STI. It's important to protect yourself both by using condoms and by using lube. Testing and keeping yourself up-to-date with what's going on with your body is important too.

Getting tested is fairly straightforward depending on what kind of sex you're having, and usually only requires swabs or a blood or urine test.

One other important health consideration to mention: whether you're pre- or post-top surgery, check for lumps every once in a while. Breast cancer is still a possibility, whatever your gender!

Finally, I'd like to talk about something that makes me really uncomfortable: the sexual fetishization of trans people. There are some people out there who actively look for trans people to have sex with. That's fine if the trans person knows and is happy about being propositioned in that way, but I personally don't want someone using me for my body like that—there's a risk that I'd be having sex with someone who doesn't see me as I truly am. Some people with trans fetishes don't consider trans women as actual women or vice versa. To think that a trans person is not the gender they identify as is twisted, and I hate that mindset. Most fetishes, like foot or latex fetishes, are harmless because they aren't oppressing anyone—you can't offend a foot. But I don't want people looking at my identity as a kinky sex object. I'm a person with a life and emotions. My transition is serious.

Overall, sex and intimacy for trans people can be as simple or as complicated as it needs to be. Communication is always key for all parties involved, but the main thing to remember is that sex can be great, even if you're trans!

19

MAKING VIDEOS

I've put myself
out there on
the internet
to be "that
trans guy."

I've been posting videos online to my YouTube channel TheRealAlexBertie since I was about thirteen. Admittedly, there aren't many videos left from my younger years—I've listed most as private because they included my birth name, were irrelevant or incorrect, or just plain embarrassing. One of my really early videos in 2008 was titled "The egg murder." I drew a face on an egg, put it in a bowl, and stabbed it with a fork. Yes—quality content. It's so funny to be able to look back at old videos and see myself at fourteen, babbling on about nothing, stumbling over my words, and being absolutely clueless to the world. I call this my "fluffy phase."

As you can guess, those videos didn't really propel me to fortune and fame. The first real hint of a following came when I posted my coming-out story. This was back when coming-out stories weren't guaranteed one million views, but were instead just you pushing out an incredibly personal thing into a mostly unused part of the internet. It was a long video with no editing, filmed directly from my shitty webcam, as I awkwardly explained my sexuality and how others reacted at school at the time. For some reason, a few hundred people thought it would be a good idea to subscribe. Before long, I was uploading weekly videos talking about anything I felt like.

I definitely still featured videos with pretty weird stuff. When I was fifteen, I bought condoms for the first time. Extra small ones. From a pound store. With my lesbian friend. We both looked horrendously young, so I can't even imagine what was going through the shop assistant's mind. We bought them to blow them up like balloons and set them free in front of a church for a YouTube video!

My first packer is something I'll remember for the rest of my life.

I bought it when I was seventeen from an online sex shop. It was a 3.5-inch "Mr. Limpy," which is a really common first packer. You're not allowed to buy sex toys unless you're over eighteen in the UK, so the whole process of buying it online and praying that it came in discreet packaging was really scary. I remember my mum asking what it was when it came and I lied, telling her it was stickers. She definitely didn't believe me!

It took a while to find my "thing."

I brought the box up to my room and found some free mints and lube inside, along with an incredibly squishy, stretchy prosthetic penis. I'd never got up close and personal with a penis before, so it was definitely a new experience. I ended up putting it in a locked steel box and hiding the key for months before I finally had the courage to use it. Later, I spray-painted it gold. I was making a video called "Uses for Packers" where I gave the viewer alternative uses for packers if they didn't want to put them in their pants. The gold penis was my proudly DIYed dick trophy!

It took a while to find my "thing," but over the last few years, my content has begun to revolve around LGBTQ+ topics. My hope is that I help, inform, and educate anyone curious enough to watch. In December 2014, I began a series called The Quest to Alex's Beard to document every step of my journey through the health care system to transition. I stuck to it, updating my subscribers on every appointment and letter leading up to April 2016 when I finally started

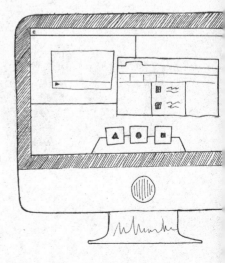

The quest is definitely NOT over.

testosterone. I can't begin to explain how amazing it felt to have so many people out there offering me support and advice during the hardest moments. The quest is definitely not over; I plan to have the series follow my journey through my further changes on T and beyond to really show what a trans person has to go through to reach happiness.

The trans community has grown so much on YouTube. It's an incredible platform for sharing transitions and being able to document the changes that come with it.

Many people choose to upload things like voice comparisons, monthly updates, and so much more. It's great to be able to learn about trans stuff from real people speaking about their own lives rather than a cold article online that might have questionable credentials. For me, the best part is being able to read comments from people around the world at different stages of transition, learning how they're progressing on their journey and working through their particular challenges.

It's very easy to view an audience as just a bunch of numbers on the screen, but it all started to feel very real when I attended my first ever YouTube gathering in 2014 called Summer in the City (SitC).

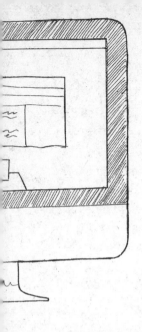

I had around 50,000 subscribers at the time and was somehow found by Jazza, an incredibly cool guy hosting an LGBTQ+ panel at the event. Just a few weeks before the event, he invited me to be a part of it, and very uncharacteristically, I said yes. Actually being there on the day, surrounded by other creators like the incredible Tyler Oakley, who I had admired for years, was my first exposure to YouTube culture.

For a little guy with a squeaky voice from a small village in the middle of nowhere, it was fucking amazing.

I've been to SitC every year since and it's always the highlight of my year. I get to meet hundreds of viewers, see my fellow creators, and get to spend time with my best friends.

When people recognize me on the street or at an event, they often only know me as the online personality I put forward, so sometimes things can get a little awkward. I do try to just be myself online, rather than being overexcited or dramatic just for views, but it's really hard to tell what other people think I'm like. In reality, I'm very quiet. There have been situations where someone will recognize me in public, we'll both say "Hey," and then...just stand there in silence.

Eventually they say, "Well, it was nice meeting you!" and excuse themselves. I swear I'm not antisocial, just more of a listener!

I often think about my "place" on YouTube in comparison to other creators. Why am I there? How long will I be around for?

After all, I'm not the most technically sophisticated YouTuber: I make unscripted videos in my bedroom, rambling on about myself with minimal editing, and I have no desire to upgrade my equipment. But hopefully my aim of being genuine runs through all my videos. I try just to be straightforward in my approach, but every now and then I do find myself thinking, *Oh, if I put "transgender" in the title, this video will get more views!* I've learned that there's a time and a place for dropping the "T-bomb," and I'm not going to call a baking video "TRANSGENDER MAN BAKES COOKIES!" just for the sake of it. What does being trans have to do with baking cookies? Instead, I save it for videos that need it in the title, like a video with my mum I called "Transgender son and his mum," where I was asking my mum questions about being the parent of a trans kid.

It can sometimes be difficult (and a little scary) having a sensitive topic like transliness at the center of my content. Offending someone is the opposite of what I want to achieve, but it can happen. I've learned that when I'm talking about any given topic, be it LGBTQ+ stuff, mental health stuff, and so on, I have to make it perfectly clear that what I'm saying is my opinion, from my personal experience, and that not everyone may feel the same.

I can't go around telling people all trans men have surgery and go on hormones because some don't, and if those trans men were to see me misrepresenting them, they'd be upset.

I never want to accidentally make someone feel bad about themselves or invalidate their identity entirely.

The weird beauty of the internet is that if you screw up, Tumblr will tell you. In a nutshell, Tumblr is a blogging website with a huge variety of content posted by users from across the globe. Literally anything you can think of, including trans stuff, is up there. It also has a reputation for being full of "social justice warriors" who promote political correctness to the extreme. I think that's too harsh, because those "warriors" are often dismissed as people who are very sensitive and get butthurt over small things, but we need people who call us out. The way I see it, if you're going to put yourself out there and talk about

i NEVER want TO ACCiDENTALLY make SOMEONE feel BAD about THEMSELVES.

I've done some questionable things that I now regret.

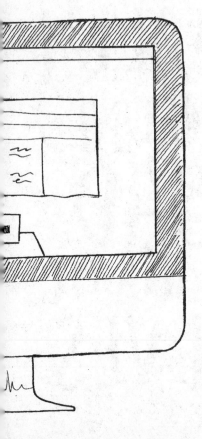

sensitive subjects like mental health or politics, claiming to be a source of education, you need to have your facts straight and be open to taking in feedback and new information from your audience.

I've done some questionable things that I now regret. One of those was being insensitive toward people who have had bottom surgery. When I was sixteen and not thinking about the words I was using and how they might make others feel, I said I wasn't interested in bottom surgery because "it wasn't perfected yet." I was grossly uneducated about the procedures available, didn't realize how offensive that statement was to those who'd had it done, and completely forgot the fact that there's no such thing as perfect. Perfection is subjective, so what I should've said was "Personally, I'm not happy with the results available yet." It's honest, but it makes clear that it's only my opinion. I wish I had been more mindful of what I said back then!

I also used to brand my content as information for and about trans people as a whole, when in reality I only spoke

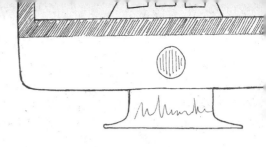

about things for and about trans men, because that's what I know. People picked up on this and were upset that I didn't speak about issues relating to other identities such as nonbinary or trans women. That's when I started being more mindful of the language I used, making sure I specified my area as "trans men" instead of just saying "trans people." It wouldn't have been fair for me to start talking about other identities, because I don't have the right to. I have no firsthand experience with those struggles, so I'm not going to steal anyone's thunder.

Unfortunately, not everyone in our community has the same attitude, and recently there's been an uproar about cis people within LGBTQ+ YouTube trying to talk on behalf of trans people.

If I can sit here and say that one trans person shouldn't speak for another because we're not all the same, imagine how important it is for cis people not to speak for trans people.

It's okay to be a trans ally, but it's essential to let the people being oppressed take the spotlight when talking about their issues.

Something I have always known but was afraid to admit for the longest time is that I don't know everything about each different sexuality and gender identity. The fact is that over my last three to four years on the internet, conversations and views on those topics have really accelerated, leading to an explosion of new terms.

That's amazing, and I'm so glad people are finally finding not just words to describe themselves, but whole communities who feel the same way.

Being a prominent trans figure online has meant that people kind of assume that I know everything about everything, which has made it incredibly difficult for me to reach out and try to learn. The person I really look up to on YouTube is Ash Hardell. They make videos about gender and sexuality (among other things) and must have dedicated a huge amount of time to researching and keeping up with LGBTQ+ terms. I mean, they wrote a book called *The ABCs of LGBT+*, so they kind of had to, but I look up to Ash very much. We actually collaborated on a video at the start of 2017 where I asked if they could educate me on things outside of my little FTM bubble, which ended up being so fantastic and eye-opening.

So no matter who you are, LGBTQ+ or not, it's understandable that you don't know everything there is to know. I don't think anybody does! What's important is that you learn from your mistakes and try your best to do your research so you're aware of why what you said could have been hurtful. Also, don't be afraid to call yourself out and ask questions! I do this all the time and can happily say that I'd rather admit ignorance, shock my audience, and then learn about a topic than pretend to know everything and get called out when I screw up.

Transition can easily sit at the front of your mind as a result of dysphoria, having to battle with the health care system or just because of your social circles. Adding a constant online "trans persona" to the list made it even harder to forget. I can't ever really have a day off where my transition is completely in the back of my mind because I always need to go on to YouTube, Twitter, Tumblr, or Facebook to read through messages from people needing advice and try to help them.

I love what I do and over time trans topics have just become a normal thing to talk about, but when I've been in the depths of dysphoria, it's been difficult to face making a video or going online to chat.

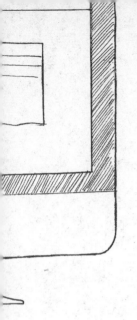

When people find out I'm transgender, sometimes that's all they can think about me. Being trans is a huge part of my identity, and I know that I've put myself out there on the internet to be "that trans guy," making videos related to gender and transitioning. But it does mean that the rest of my personality kind of gets drained away. If that's how I have to label myself for people to find me in the huge online universe, then so be it. The problem comes when people in real life think of me in the same way. In real life, I'm not a walking encyclopedia of trans knowledge like in my videos.

Being trans is only one part of who I am, and it took me a while to realize that after I came out.

I try not to get too defensive about people "outing" me, because a simple Google search of my name will do the same thing, but it's nice having that power within your own hands. In my case, sometimes people don't even realize they're doing it. I've had people I know start talking about my YouTube channel to their friends right in front of me. It's weird; as proud as I am about my videos, they're trans-related and I don't always want people to know that part of me right away. Usually, the person being told will get really excited so they'll pull up my channel page. Nine times out of ten, I jump in front of the screen and warn them to watch in private, since everything I talk about is really personal. (Not to mention that watching my old videos around other people makes me cringe!)

I make videos to help people and connect with my community.

So far I think it's going pretty well, but I'm not relying on the YouTube thing to last forever or propel me into something else, as much as I'd love it to. I left school and studied to be a graphic designer for four years at the same time as making videos. I was always so worried about the future of my channel after I got a nine-to-five job, but it's all pretty much the same—although I occasionally miss an upload because my weekends are now hectic!

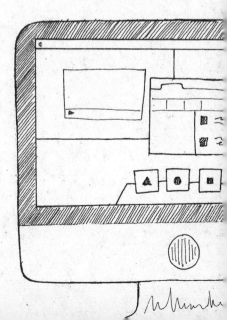

20

JOB HUNTING

Oh my God, I think he's going to offer me the job!

I'm very open about being trans, but I do think carefully about who I tell, and it's definitely not the first thing I say when I meet someone. It's not like I walk into a room and shout, "HELLO, I'M A MAN WITH A VAGINA." Usually, I find it easier to make friends with someone if they know me as a person before they find out I'm trans. That way, they don't assume anything before they meet me and there's nothing clouding their judgment. It gives us both time to actually find out what we like about each other, and for me to gain trust in them. However, I have found that my transition can be a great way to get to know someone quickly—it's a way of trading really personal information, making you instantly closer to someone. I did this when I started my current job and told the people who worked near me that I was trans. It helped my new colleagues feel like they knew me, and things didn't feel so awkward from then on. It was also a great conversation starter because I can go on all day about trans stuff; it definitely helped me to come out of my shell.

My first job was a disaster. It was at an extremely popular fast food restaurant when I was sixteen. I came out as trans in my interview—well, sort of. My only questions to the interviewer were "Are your uniforms gender-specific?" and "Can I use my preferred name on my nametag?" Funnily enough, they got the picture!

Even though my name hadn't yet been legally changed, nobody referred to me as female—and I was given a nametag with the right name and a guy's uniform.

I quit on my second day. Not because of my trans status, but because I suck at customer service and remembering orders. There may also have been an incident with an ice cream machine going rogue, overflowing all over the floor…

In September 2016, I began hunting for my first step on the career ladder. I'm terrible because I always try to turn things that I love into a job—I've always had the mindset that I don't want to hate what I do for a living. Art is my passion, so I soon settled on the dream of becoming a graphic designer. I love being able to put my creativity into earning money.

There's never really a dull moment when you're trans, and finding a job was no different. In every

My online presence loomed over my head like a huge black cloud.

job application, my online presence loomed over my head like a huge black cloud, ready to piss all over everything. YouTube is a huge part of my life, and people can find out everything about me just by googling my name. In my adult life I've never really had a terrible reaction to someone finding out that I'm trans, but that doesn't mean I don't still wish I had the choice to keep it private. Don't get me wrong—I'm incredibly proud of what I do online, but it's very easy for someone to find me and get all these ideas about who I am before they've even met me.

So essentially I had two choices: hide it and pray a potential employer didn't stumble across it, or own it. I chose to own it—in fact, I put it on my resume! I was amazed to see how many employers value video-editing and social media knowledge alongside graphic design, so my YouTube channel ended up landing me multiple job opportunities. I also had lots of trans-based graphic design in my portfolio, which was the perfect excuse to come out within the first ten minutes of each interview.

I strongly believe that there are certain people who just need to know that you're trans.

Being trans can be difficult in part because it makes you stand out from other people, but in this situation, that was a huge advantage. Being open isn't for everybody, but all the pieces kind of fell into place for me to make my trans status beneficial.

I strongly believe that there are certain people who just need to know that you're trans. Your potential boss is probably one of them. I knew that I was going to need flexibility within my job from day one to attend medical appointments and eventually have surgery. Within my first few days on trial shifts, I mentioned needing time off, saying that I'd make the hours up in whatever way I could. My job ended up being designing marketing material at a school, which is kind of perfect. The hours are restricted to the semester, so any time I need off I can work back within school holidays. Let's work this out: psychotherapy appointments, doctor appointments, blood tests, testosterone shots, and surgery...That's two days off every three months, plus two days off every six months, and a whopping eleven days off for surgery. I think being honest about my circumstances really helped my employer to understand that the appointments are important, but don't affect my commitment to the job.

If anything, it was my YouTube channel that caused the most drama in the application process rather than my trans status. I had two interviews. After the second one, they gave me a date by which I'd hear from them, no matter what. That day came and went, and I started to give up hope, overanalyzing everything I'd said in the interviews that might have sounded bad. But finally, I got the call. The head of marketing for the school sounded a little apprehensive over the phone, saying that he had to talk to me about something. My mind went to all the questions he could ask about my gender. It was a huge relief when he started talking about my YouTube channel instead, saying that if I were to get the job, I wouldn't be able to talk about where I worked and that I'd need to behave appropriately online. I squirmed as he read out a few of my more "colorful" video titles, but to be honest all I could think about was *Oh my God, I think he's going to offer me the job!* One background check and a few video-title changes later, I was at the desk of my first design job.

I'm out to a number of people at work, but I only told three of them directly myself. The rest heard

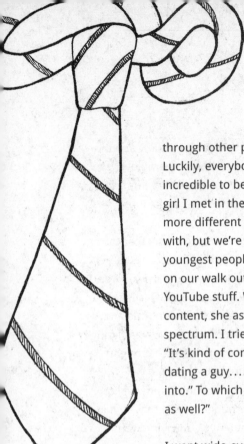

through other people or from finding me online. Luckily, everybody is really respectful and it's incredible to be in such an accepting place. There's a girl I met in the office called Rhiann, who couldn't be more different from the people I normally get along with, but we're both the same age and both the youngest people who work at the school. One day on our walk out of work, we started talking about my YouTube stuff. When I mentioned making LGBTQ+ content, she asked where exactly I fell on that spectrum. I tried to be vague by awkwardly saying, "It's kind of complicated...I...um...well...I'm dating a guy....But that's not the only letter I fall into." To which she responded calmly, "So—the T as well?"

I went wide-eyed and said, "Yeah! How did you...?" Rhiann is studying law at university, and it turns out she was thinking about looking at law surrounding transgender issues for her dissertation. How does life throw people together like this?!

It was a complete blessing and I instantly felt more relaxed because I knew that I didn't have to explain myself or try to educate her on trans stuff.

I'm aware that as far as trans people go, I'm very privileged. I'm a white educated male with family support, a roof over my head, and a job.

However, for a lot of trans people, finding employment is difficult due to discrimination and prejudice.

So many transgender people (especially trans women) end up either homeless or turning to sex work to put food on the table. Sex work for trans people can be lucrative, but it can also be incredibly dangerous. There's a high risk of violence, STIs (trans women are fifty times more likely to contract HIV due to poor access to health services), negative mental health effects, and addiction—all resulting from sex work.

I'm not judging anyone's life choices; I just want to point out that this is a reality for many people. For a trans person, it's a very easy situation to find yourself in. If someone's family kicks them out after they come out as trans, and they can't find a job due to transphobic employers, there are few other options. It's so important for society to make progress in their knowledge and acceptance of transgender people.

21

OUR PLACE IN THE WORLD

Hate never wins.

The UK has legislation (the 2010 Equality Act) stating that you cannot discriminate against someone based on gender identity. That doesn't mean it never happens—transphobic hate crimes increased by 170 percent in 2016—but we do at least have some sort of legal protection in Britain. That isn't the case in many other places around the world. In plenty of countries, an employer can flat-out refuse to hire you because you're trans. It's disgusting, but it's only one of the many hate crimes that trans people face globally every day.

Between 2008 and 2014, there were 1,731 *recorded* cases of trans people being murdered worldwide. Remember, those are just the recorded cases. Think about the many countries that have anti-LGBTQ+ laws and a motive to cover up their own statistics.

One of the most recent high-profile legal issues was the "anti-trans bathroom bill." Yes, it's as ridiculous as it sounds. This bill, which is also known as the Public Facilities Privacy & Security Act, passed in North Carolina in 2016. It prevents people from using a public bathroom that doesn't align with the sex on their birth certificate. That's incredibly harmful to the trans community, because it can be really difficult and costly to get your birth certificate changed—in fact, in North Carolina, you have to have had sex reassignment surgery in order to change your certificate. There are two huge problems here:

(A) that surgery costs thousands of dollars, meaning a lot of people who might want it can't afford it, and (B) not all trans people want surgery in the first place. The bill has been dubbed the "most anti-LGBTQ+ legislation" in the United States.

Another outrageous story occurred a few years ago. Russia has a reputation for not being supportive of LGBTQ+ rights, but the law passed in 2015 took its government to a new low. It compiled a long list of criteria that would exclude people from being able to drive, including certain mental and physical disabilities, as well as what they referred to as "personality disorders."

Those excluded ranged from pathological gamblers and kleptomaniacs to those who partake in pedophilia, sadomasochism, exhibitionism, and fetishism. Oh, and don't forget—trans people!

Russia has an incredibly high number of car accidents per year, so it's understandable that they were looking for a way to reduce it...but wow, did they look in the wrong place! The only reason I'd be more prone to a car accident than a cis person is if my prosthetic penis were to somehow fall down my pant leg and get stuck under the brake pedal.

There's a high chance that I'd be attacked or even murdered for being trans.

Thanks to the TV show *Orange Is the New Black*, I think a lot about what it'd be like if I were to be sent to prison. The show is about a women's prison in the United States, and one of the characters is a MTF trans lady named Sophia (played by trans actor Laverne Cox). I'm not planning on going to prison any time soon, but it didn't stop me from trying to do some digging into where I'd be sent.

To be honest, both options terrify me. Going to a female prison would completely invalidate my identity because I'd be the only guy there. In an all-male prison, I'd 100 percent be at risk of being raped. In either situation, I'd be extremely vulnerable to the actions of other inmates or prison guards—there's a high chance that I'd be attacked or even murdered for being trans.

Some prisons do put LGBTQ+ inmates into protective custody, which usually means solitary confinement. Even though that makes trans inmates safer, 44 percent of trans men and 40 percent of trans women in

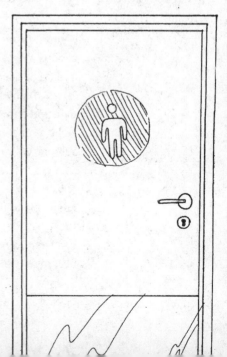

protective custody have said they still experienced some form of harassment. There's also a high chance that trans inmates in solitary confinement would miss out on health care services, education programs, social activities, visitors, and privileges like watching TV or exercising. *Orange Is the New Black* included a story arc about Sophia being denied hormone treatment due to prison-funding cuts. When I looked into the stats on this, unsurprisingly, 44 percent of US transgender inmates report being denied their hormone treatments.

It's my personal belief that access to health care is one of our basic human rights, and that treatment for gender dysphoria falls into that.

Without proper treatment, dysphoria can have a serious mental health impact, so by denying a trans inmate this service, you're not teaching them a lesson. If anything, you're adding to their anger or pain and encouraging them to turn to illegal activities while in prison to distract themselves from their self-hatred.

Thanks to the internet, the trans community has been able to unite across the world and support those fighting against prejudice. Social media has been a great educator on trans issues, and everyone of all ages is now able to access important information. That probably has a lot to do with why UK gender identity clinics are straining to accommodate a rapidly increasing number of patients. It's bad for wait times, but great to see more people seeking help for their dysphoria.

There are all sorts of online organizations and businesses that help trans people too. There are publications like *Hudson's FTM Resource Guide* and websites that sell trans-specific items like packers, binders, and special boxers for trans men dealing with a menstrual cycle. There are clothing companies that donate their proceeds to surgery funds or trans charities, and even organizations that collect and donate essentials such as binders for free to those who can't afford them. I love the internet!

Unfortunately, the huge online trans community frequently gets accused of brainwashing kids.

Critics even make out that being trans is a new trend. Education isn't brainwashing, because nobody online tells kids that they are trans—they're telling people what it means to be trans. And while the internet is great for spreading awareness about topics like different uses of pronouns, it also encourages people to make fun of the community, especially those with nonbinary identities.

Society has A LOT of WORK TO do on EQUALITY and TRANS RIGHTS.

The term "snowflake" is thrown around a lot, and is used against someone deemed to consider themselves unique or who is too easily offended by people.

I've seen a lot of people who identify outside of the gender binary be called a "snowflake" and it's just infuriating. These people are valid. Not everyone identifies as either male or female 100 percent of the time. *ARGH!*

Society has a lot of work to do on equality and trans rights, but with the amount of exposure our community is getting in the media at the moment, I think we're well on our way. You just have to look back through history to see that marginalized groups like women and people of color had to endure horrific times before things got better. Don't get me wrong—the battle is far from over for both of those groups, but the progression of their rights movements is really encouraging. I just don't see how people can discriminate against a minority and think they will prevail. Hate never wins.

22

A MESSAGE FROM MY MUM

I thought it would be helpful to all the parents out there if they could read what my mum has to say about having a transgender child. The following is written by my mum, Michelle Bertie.

Alex has given me some simple questions to help focus my writing. My aim is to answer them honestly. So, from the time Alex asked me to contribute to the book, I've chosen not to read anything else about transgender kids and their parents. My words are based on my memories of our experiences—I want to be as forthcoming and truthful as possible about what members of my family and I went through. Okay, here goes:

Did Alex show early signs of being uncomfortable with his gender during childhood?

I have looked through countless photos and home videos to look for clues about whether Alex was uncomfortable with his gender when growing up. Despite many hours spent trying to guess what was going through his mind in each moment, I have to honestly say I don't know. Throughout those photo albums and in my memories, Alex just seemed like a happy and cheerful child wearing what he wanted and doing what he wanted.

Before Alex was born, we bought white, lemon, and lime clothes. We felt they were good neutral choices,

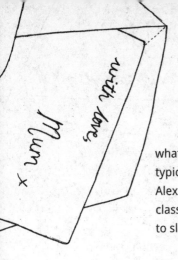

With love,
Mum x

whatever the gender of our baby. His nursery had typically pink walls with white frilly bedsheets, but Alex wore lots of differently colored clothes and had classic gender-neutral toys. I remember rocking him to sleep in my lap, singing the words "my baby girl."

When Alex first started primary school, he wore a standard pinafore. But when we moved and he went to a new school, he was adamant that he did not want to wear a skirt—he insisted he wanted to wear pants. The school allowed this, so I reluctantly agreed. Many of the other girls also wore pants during the winter, so it didn't seem unusual. But come summer, Alex was still not happy at the thought of wearing a dress; he preferred polo shirts and pants instead.

Despite having Barbies and makeup sets, Alex usually chose toy cars, Play-Doh, and Lego.

He enjoyed playing with both boys and girls, but always ended up having more fun with the boys.

During his tween years, Alex continued to wear track pants and hoodies. At the time I thought nothing of it, since I lived in my jeans or work pants and never wore flowery outfits either. Still, dressing up for World Book Day was always difficult. Alex never wanted to be a princess, always choosing to be a surfer or a mad professor. It made me frustrated and confused that Alex had no interest in anything feminine. Sometimes I blamed myself for always being at work—I wondered if I wasn't providing enough of a feminine influence. But then I thought back to my own childhood, when I loved playing with cars and preferred my male friends. I decided nothing was out of the ordinary.

When Alex started middle school, he wanted to wear a shirt and tie, which was one of the uniform options.

I also started to notice that Alex would always end up in the boys' section in the shops; he could never quite find anything in the right color or fit in the girls' section.

He would never consider shoes with straps or laces, and if I suggested buckles or bows, I was given *the look*, as if to say *Are you crazy?* I often questioned his attitude, but Alex would just stomp off and ignore me, which I found really upsetting. I had long conversations with his dad, asking him to encourage Alex to visit the girls' section since my opinion wasn't wanted. Despite his calm approach, Alex's dad didn't have any more luck. I felt lost about what to do, often asking close friends for their opinion.

I don't think they knew what to say either, except for "Does it matter?" My response would always be "No, I suppose not."

In truth, I wanted Alex to have clothes that he would wear happily. But I was also conscious of other people's reactions—everyone always said that he was a tomboy.

At that age, Alex mostly had male friends. We explained to him that they might soon have girlfriends and that he might feel left out—or that his friends' girlfriends might get jealous. Sadly, we turned out to be right. Alex became quieter than usual at home and would rarely want to talk to me about any trouble he was having, often shutting himself in his room. All he cared about was discussing the latest Photoshop program or the latest edition of a video game. I felt Alex was a lot closer to his dad, and I missed the close bond we had once had. Looking back, I wonder if that was Alex's way of connecting with his male self.

On one occasion at middle school, Alex came home absolutely furious. Once he'd calmed down, we realized that he'd been in a difficult situation on the school bus. The children had been told to get on the bus, girls first. When Alex tried to get on with the girls, he was told off and asked to wait. Alex tried

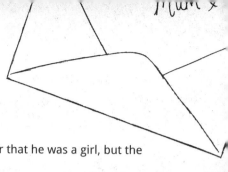

to explain to the teacher that he was a girl, but the teacher became angry.

After a long chat with Alex, I had the difficult task of taking up the issue with the school. Alex clearly often looked like a boy, wearing pants and a tie unlike the other girls who had fancy hair, makeup, and short skirts.

I was frustrated that Alex was being expected to conform to a specific gender stereotype, but at the same time I had to admit that thinking he was a boy was an easy mistake to make.

I felt very torn, and I remember trying to explain to Alex that sometimes assumptions would be made because he chose to present himself in a certain way. I was confused; he seemed to want to look like a boy, so I couldn't understand why the mistake had made him so upset. Looking back, it was an early sign that Alex had very mixed emotions about his gender.

The middle-school dance—what a nightmare that was for both Alex and me! He wanted to wear pants, but I spent a long time explaining that all the girls would be wearing dresses and that he would be bullied if he made that choice for the dance. We finally reached a compromise: a long simple black

ith love,

Mum x

dress would "do." After hours of searching, we found a suitable dress. Despite being told that he looked beautiful and had the perfect figure, Alex was clearly uncomfortable wearing it, standing with a slump and a miserable face. I felt very guilty for almost forcing Alex to comply with social expectations. I would never usually support that, but that time, I wanted to protect him from being excluded even more.

While he was getting ready for the big night, I tried to convince Alex that a little makeup would be nice. After I pretty much pinned Alex down, I managed to apply it. Big mistake. Alex had never liked makeup, and he was not happy. Nor did he like his gorgeous long blond hair, normally tied back in a low ponytail, flowing down the back of the dress. I thought Alex looked stunning, but he just felt ugly.

It came to me all of a sudden: was this for him or for me?

By the time Alex started high school, I'd made peace with the idea that he was a tomboy. I didn't feel totally at ease about how he was doing though. On the one hand, he was working hard in school, but on the other, he always seemed unhappy. We held lots of meetings at the school to discuss why other children were bullying him. We always defended Alex's right to make individual choices about his appearance, even if they didn't necessarily conform with what his classmates did.

Before long he wanted his hair cut, his gorgeous long hair. Alex had a reason: it was cut and donated to a charity for children with cancer; it all seemed perfectly justifiable.

Perhaps it was a way for him to fit in with his new friends. They all seemed to have very individual personalities, which mostly didn't worry me. My only concern was that alcohol or drugs would be Alex's next chapter. During our trips to town to drop him off to meet friends, I gave Alex stiff lectures. He always reassured me that his friends were not like that, but I still worried. I wanted him to have friends, but were they the friends he needed?

One day, one of his female friends came over with her grandma to deliver a birthday present for Alex. Although they had traveled quite far, they refused to come in. I remember the grandma thanking me for Alex being such a special friend to her granddaughter. She obviously meant more than just friends, and that set my mind thinking about Alex's sexuality. I worried. Was it a problem? Was it my business? I decided it wasn't. As it happened, around that time Alex confided in me about his sexuality himself.

To be honest, I was more concerned about him achieving good grades than what his relationship choices were.

I don't think Alex saw that as helpful; he probably thought I didn't care. I did care, but I thought his education would affect far more in his life than his sexuality would.

Toward the end of high school, I found out that Alex had made discoveries about his gender through our conversations and a letter he gave to me. I write more about my reaction to his news in my next answer, but for now let's say that all I wanted was for Alex to get through his exams. I was anxious for him to leave school with good enough results to get to college, where he could start to really be himself.

When Alex started college, I decided it was time for me to step back and let him learn to take control of his own life. He presented as male throughout college, using his new name and preferred identity—very few people knew he was trans. The party he had before going to college was much better than his middle-school dance. Alex went in clothes he had chosen himself, with the hairstyle he wanted, and didn't wear an ounce of makeup. He had no stress about conforming to the expectations of others or the related pressures of

gender dysphoria. My happy child was back: his college party photos are of a beaming Alex posing with all his friends. Finally, he was comfortable and settled and looking forward to his next chapter in life.

How have your feelings about Alex's transition changed over time?

The moment Alex told me about his gender dysphoria, I felt an incredible sense of guilt. Was it my fault? Had I done something wrong? Should I have noticed earlier? Who do I turn to? What do I do now? I felt as though I was to blame for my child being so unhappy for so long, without my even realizing. What kind of a parent did that make me? I was filled with an overwhelming sense of sadness. I felt that I had let my child down in so many ways, and I had no idea what to do or say to him and those around me.

I had met transgender people before Alex came out, but this felt very different. With the people I had met before, their transliness really didn't seem like a big deal. So why was it so hard for me to understand when it came to Alex? And why did I feel so guilty? Looking back, I think it was seeing my own child feeling upset, alone, and distraught that twanged my whole heart and made it so upsetting.

I had always wanted my child to grow up happy; this was not how I had expected parenting to be.

I think I was also partly reacting to the difficulties and discrimination I had seen other trans people encounter. Thankfully, I managed to put those thoughts at the back of my mind pretty quickly. I decided that I had to accept Alex's situation as a new experience and take it one step at a time.

I asked Alex to always be honest with me about his transition. I wanted to be able to help in any way that I could. When I found out that he was also being honest with the entire internet, I was pretty alarmed. I felt I needed to protect Alex from anyone who wasn't going to be understanding, and I was worried that Alex might be stalked or psychologically harmed by online strangers to the point of considering suicide. It was my biggest worry and I often monitored his Facebook or YouTube accounts to check for signs.

I was also very concerned about the operations that he would want and the implications they would have. I remember spending hours talking to him about medical procedures; it felt like it was all we ever talked about. On reflection, I understand why—but at the time it felt like everyday life had been lost to Alex's dysphoria and that nothing else mattered to him, which of course it didn't. I tried to understand Alex's feelings, but I also wanted him to take time and be sure that this wasn't a phase. It would be awful if he changed his mind when it was too late. Besides, it seemed to me that with the clothes he wore and his short haircut, he was already pretty much leading his life as a man. I asked him to wait before taking any big steps in his transition, and tried to explain that when he was eighteen years old and an adult, he'd be able to make his own decisions about his future.

The period after Alex changed his name was a difficult time, because I was still using his birth name to family and friends.

After eighteen years it was ingrained—and if remembering the correct name was hard, changing pronouns was even more challenging. It was also socially difficult, because I didn't want to cause Alex any offense but not everyone in our family knew about his transition at the time. Thankfully, I had had a pet name for Alex since he was a toddler: Spanner. I often used it when we were in a family setting, since it was a non-gendered term that was still very personal to Alex. However, using his new name became easier over time, with help from my friends and work colleagues; we'd laugh when I ended up

using several different names and pronouns within the same sentence.

While I wanted to support Alex's journey, I still had other family and work commitments, which were also really important.

I felt very torn; it was difficult to balance everyone else's needs with his, and to know how much to help Alex or just leave him to organize his own path.

It didn't take too long for Alex to feel ready to request access to the gender identity clinic. I offered to go along to his first doctor appointment to make sure that he was treated fairly and to show him that he was fully supported, but he said no in case questions about his family came up. When his referral letter arrived, I felt so happy for him. Alex's dream was becoming a reality and hope was in sight.

I tried hard to keep other people informed about the journey Alex was taking and was often very nervous about other people's reactions. Some people were understanding and supportive, but not everyone was. I got less bothered by that as more people learned about our situation. I just felt proud that we were able to be honest and open. When Alex started testosterone, I had some concerns. I was worried about angry outbursts caused by high testosterone levels and that if he didn't stick to a strict regime, the shots might have a negative impact on his health. We talked these issues through together, and we went through the calendar writing down all the planned shot dates and blood tests. He has maintained his regime independently ever since, and I'm very proud of his awareness and sensible approach.

When the testosterone started to take effect, I noticed Alex's changing body shape and appetite fairly quickly.

It was good to see Alex walking around more confidently after hunching for so many years, and he started to eat well too.

His voice lowered so gradually that I didn't spot it at first—I only noticed the difference when I looked back at old videos.

The most recent big step was top surgery. I had known for years that he had been binding his chest, and I'd never agreed with it—I was worried about negative side effects. Still, when Alex had asked me to adjust one of his swimsuits to act as a binder, I'd tried to help. Soon after he managed to buy a proper one, and I know it was very uncomfortable to wear for long periods of time.

For years I felt helpless, only able to offer sympathy, so when he started talking about surgery, it seemed like an obvious solution.

Nevertheless, I remember telling Alex that it might take some time for me to get used to him being topless around the house.

The wait for surgery seemed endless, but then suddenly it happened and was over in no time at all. I had booked a week off work to be an assistant and nurse, and I am so glad I did. I think any mum would feel helpless if their child underwent surgery, and I just wanted to be there for Alex. Having said that, I was probably a bit overprotective. No one else got a say—I was going to be there no matter what.

It has taken many years of patience for me to understand how Alex feels about his body and the way he thinks about himself. But now that I understand, I feel ready to take on anyone and anything that might stand in the way of my child's happiness.

What advice would you give to other parents whose child has come out as transgender?

I am by no means an expert or a counselor, so this is just my point of view. The most important thing of all is to listen to your child and try to understand how they feel about themselves and the world around them. They will probably have done lots of thinking about what they could do to make themselves feel better physically and psychologically. We all have our own perception of what is normal, but generations evolve and perceptions of "normal" change as quickly as the weather. I believe everyone has the right to be their own person however they wish.

Always try to be sensitive. In my experience, that's like walking on eggshells with iron boots, but it's important to try.

For example, be very careful when using names and pronouns. Using the wrong name is like hitting your child with a brick: it hurts! Feelings are invisible but they have a lasting effect on relationships. When our feelings are hurt or offended, we can easily shut down communication within relationships. You two know each other like no one else, and only you know how to press each other's buttons, so avoid hurting each other whenever you can.

Loneliness is a terrible feeling, whether you are a child or a parent.

Alex and I found support in different places, and we each dealt with our feelings in our own ways, but I like to think that we made it through together eventually. We often found we were talking at, rather than to, each other at first, but we persisted and always found a way to express ourselves. Alex wrote us letters, which allowed him to speak openly without interruption; I found regular trips to his room worked, as they were a time for us to clearly say whatever needed to be said. Often I simply asked Alex what I could do to help. He would say things like "Use my correct name!" or "Stop telling me to look at girls' shoes!"

Should you be afraid? I honestly think that you can only be afraid of what you don't understand. Take time to talk to different people, be they professional or otherwise. Information about transition and transgender people can be found all over the place. Friends, family, doctors, nurses, schools, support groups, and the internet can all be sources of help. The list is a long one, so use any resources you feel are right for you and your child. I have some medical experience so I was fully aware of the procedures, but I still watched videos online just to put my mind at ease.

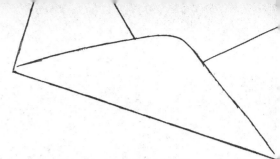

Sometimes, the best resource is your own child. The transgender world is a very different one than my own and I often ask stupid questions, but my mum always said, "If you don't ask, you will never know!" Alex frequently needed to explain LGBTQ+ terms to me that I used incorrectly by accident. We laugh at some things now and I still sometimes get reprimanded for not "getting it," but the point is that I am trying. Please try not to be afraid of asking questions. Remember, a transgender person is often so lost that they may come across as angry and hateful in their answers, but it's not your fault. They are just trying to find themselves and need a lot of reassurance and support from you to do it. As parents, we are expected to have all the answers, but we are only human ourselves.

Parenting does not come with a manual for every eventuality—as soon as you accept this, you are on to a winner.

When it comes to telling other people, just keep communicating. Never give up, even when it seems hopeless. Try not to hold a grudge if someone doesn't understand. Everyone is entitled to their own opinion and it may not match your own. Instead, give them as much information as you can without trying to change their mind—they might come around themselves when they understand the situation a bit more.

Alex is a much happier person now and trots around like the king of the jungle. He is still the kind, considerate person he always was and he always looks out for the other guy. I am very proud of him. Times can be hard and people can be harsh during transition, but with a little help and understanding, neither of you will ever be alone.

—Michelle Bertie

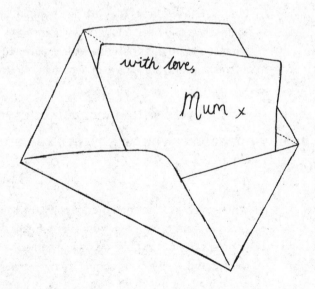

WITH A little help AND understanding, NEITHER of you will BE alone.

23
ACCEPTING TRANS PEOPLE

It means giving them peace of mind by respecting who they are.

It can't have been easy for my parents to try to seem supportive and accepting while still leaving me to be independent and do everything on my own. That's why I wanted to come up with some tips on how to show acceptance and respect to a trans person, be it your kid, family member, friend, lover, colleague, or a complete stranger.

1. If they have a new name, use it. No matter how hard it is for you, you should at least try. If you accidentally use the wrong name, correct yourself and apologize. Doing this shows that you understand what you said was potentially hurtful, and the trans person will appreciate it as long as it's genuine. My birth name carries a lot of pain with it and I feel really, really shitty if I hear somebody say it to me. If somebody knows I've changed my name and they still use my birth name, it's a huge slap in the face and completely ignores everything I've been through in my transition to be happy.

2. If you don't know their birth name, don't ask. Generally speaking, most trans people don't want others knowing their birth name because it's irrelevant. If they do tell you, or somehow you find out, for the love of God, don't go spreading it around. Nobody else has the right to tell people but them.

3. Don't "out" them. Don't tell anyone else they're trans. Even if you're a proud parent! It's a very personal thing and it's not a cheap piece of gossip. By telling other people, you could be putting their safety at risk—even though society is getting more accepting every day, there are still people out there who want to see harm come to our community. It could also make people treat them differently. For example, I'd hate it if my manager at work thought it was okay to tell everybody that I was trans, because I don't want anyone to treat me weirdly or think it's okay to ask personal or invasive questions…which brings me on to my next point.

4. Don't ask invasive questions. Please don't ask me what my genitals are or how I have sex. It's just so rude—if you're not the one I'm having sex with, you don't need to know.

5. Share in their happiness. Try to be a part of the positive aspects of their transition. This will bring you both closer together and show them that you understand the importance of their journey. For example, my parents came with me when I had top surgery. I'll always remember the moments of nervousness and excitement that we shared. It was the ultimate sign of love and acceptance!

6. Be there for them in the bad times. Trans people can suffer from really dramatic mood swings as a result of dysphoria, and sometimes we'll hit rock bottom. There are no foolproof ways to make them

Let them know that they have people around them who care.

feel better; a lot of the time, there's nothing you can do but be there. When I get into a bad place, sometimes I want somebody to listen to me rant or engage in angry bitching sessions about how bad life is. Sometimes I just want somebody to distract me from whatever is bringing me down. All you can do is listen to them and try your best to be what they need in any given moment. But I can tell you from experience that if you're not trans, trying to tell them that you "know how they feel" will get you into trouble. You can't really compare anything to dysphoria, not even on a scale of "hurt," so it's best just not to go there.

7. Be friendly! A lot of trans people can feel pretty lonely, especially just after coming out, so it's important to let them know that they have people around them who care. You might even want to suggest they attend an LGBTQ+ group—talking to people in similar situations can sometimes be really helpful. I go to a trans group at least once a month so I feel

connected to my community again. It's nice to be able to ask questions and share stories!

8. Act normal. Most of us don't want special treatment—we just want to live our lives like everybody else. While it's nice to feel interesting, a trans person isn't a science project, so please don't stare! You'd be surprised by how many times I've had people staring at me until finally blurting out, "You would never even be able to tell you were trans!" As flattering as that is, keep it to yourself.

9. Do your research. While it's okay to ask a trans person questions, they're not your only source of knowledge. Use the internet to find out more—it can also help you avoid accidentally saying something hurtful or offensive.

10. Don't assume their gender. This one only really applies if you don't know the person very well and their gender identity isn't clear. Try asking, "Which pronouns do you use?" This is a more respectful and sensitive way of asking how they identify. It shows that you understand that someone's gender expression doesn't always match up with their identity.

Ultimately, accepting or supporting a trans person doesn't mean holding their hand on the way to the gender identity clinic or being the first person they see after surgery. It means giving them peace of mind by respecting who they are.

It's not all about gaining acceptance from other people; you also have to learn to accept yourself. Most trans people in the UK have access to surgery and hormones through the public health care system, but the wait for those treatments can be long. Until then, you have to just learn to let go. I figured out my gender identity at about fifteen and didn't go on hormones until I turned twenty, so for a long time I had to figure out little ways to make do. You need to look at yourself and take advantage of your traits that line up to your gender identity. I've got a pretty square jaw, so in pictures I made sure the light was right and I showed that off. My legs were also seriously hairy pre-T, so I took advantage of that and I wore shorts sometimes to make myself feel better. It's really hard to love your body when you have bad dysphoria, but if you can pick just one thing about yourself that you do like, you'll get a huge confidence boost.

24

THE OTHER SIDE

I'm going
to live
the best and
happiest life
I possibly can.

So here I am, just living life. I'm not on wait lists or counting down the days till surgery. And now that I'm on hormones, my mind is a lot quieter than it used to be. When I was completely filled with dysphoria, my thoughts seemed to crash around my head like a marching band. But now I feel complete, like I can finally begin living and look to the future.

The thing is, I'm not sure what that future looks like. Now that the majority of my little goals have been accomplished, where do I go from here? Sure, at some point I'm going to need a hysterectomy, but that's not exactly something to work toward. I graduated college and got a job, so that's done, but the only thing I can think of now is to eventually move out. It's weird, I have to look around at other people my age to get some sort of idea about where I should be going in life next. After all, while everybody else was learning to drive, I was battling the health care system. While they were out clubbing, I was in my room trying to keep myself together. Perhaps it's just about relaxing and having fun for a while.

Writing this book has been the craziest experience. I've never sat down and thought about everything that's happened from start to finish. More than anything, it's really put things into perspective and made me realize how lucky I am. Lucky to have access to trans health care, a supportive family, and of course my amazing followers on the internet.

Without those three things, I don't think I could do what I do online, and I certainly wouldn't have had the opportunity to create something like this, so thank you.

Moving forward, I'm going to live the best and happiest life I possibly can, and I encourage all of my trans family to try to do the same. As a community and as individuals, we are so strong. We fight to be ourselves through the intolerance of others, despite the dysphoria that can drag us down.

Even after starting hormones and having top surgery, I still experience dysphoria. It's not as constant as it once was though it gets bad after a trigger, such as hearing someone use my birth name. Luckily, I'm a lot more experienced in dealing with dysphoria now than I once was, and just knowing that it will eventually dissolve is comforting. I try to think of dysphoria like a cloud: it can go from being wispy and hardly there to black and menacing. But you'll never have the same cloud floating above your head for too long, and eventually it'll pass to reveal a beautiful blue sky.

Let's prove to the world that we can live long, happy, and successful lives. If you can take just one thing from this book, let it be to not waste another second of your life stuck being someone you're not. There's a life beyond waiting for treatment or acceptance. We only get one shot at life, so get out there.

Do whatever you need to do to be

happy.

GLOSSARY

Here's a list of terms to remember. Some of them weren't mentioned in the book, but all are good to know!

Disclaimer: While I've done my best to break down these terms, they might not be 100 percent accurate. Different people explain things in different ways, and terms evolve over time.

AFAB and AMAB: Acronyms meaning "assigned/designated female at birth" or "assigned/designated male at birth." These terms are preferred over saying someone is "biologically male/female" or "born male/female."

Ally: Someone who supports a community that they're not a part of.

Androgynous: Being more ambiguous with the way you physically express your gender, displaying both masculine and feminine traits.

Androsexual: Being primarily attracted to males and/or masculinity.

Aromantic: An aromantic person doesn't feel an emotional need to be with someone else in a romantic relationship. It's a myth that an aromantic person cannot feel love—love comes in many forms, not just romantic.

Asexuality: The lack of or low desire to engage in sexual activity.

Binding: Flattening of the chest using different forms of compression.

Biological sex: The characteristics of your body (internal and external genitals, hormones, and chromosomes) that assign you to male or female. In some places, intersex is also legally recognized as a third sex.

Bottom surgery: Genital surgery.

Cisgender: Someone whose gender identity matches their biological sex.

Coming out: Disclosing your sexuality or gender identity.

Demisexual: Describes someone with little ability to experience sexual attraction until a romantic or emotional connection has been made.

Detransitioning: When someone decides to begin the process of reversing their original transition.

Drag king or queen: A form of exaggerated, theatrical, or performative gender presentation. Participating in drag does not invalidate your gender identity.

FTM: Describes a female-to-male trans person.

Gender: *see* Gender identity

Gender binary: The classification of gender into only two categories: male and female.

Gender dysphoria: A feeling of discomfort toward yourself as a result of your biological sex.

Gender expression: The way you present yourself, through signifiers such as the way you act, talk, and dress.

Gender identity: How you feel on the inside in relation to the gender binary. Someone might feel male, female, something else, everything, or nothing at all. It doesn't necessarily match with the way someone presents on the outside and is separate from their biological sex.

Gynesexual: Being primarily attracted to females and/or femininity.

HRT: Hormone replacement therapy.

Intersex: Describes someone whose genitals or chromosomes do not conform to the typical definitions of male or female.

LGBTQ+: Lesbian, gay, bisexual, trans, queer/questioning, and other sexuality and gender identities.

Misgendered: When someone is referred to as a gender identity that they don't associate with.

MTF: Describes a male-to-female trans person.

Nonbinary: Describes someone who identifies outside of the gender binary.

Packing: Putting something in your underwear to give the appearance of a bulge.

Pansexual: Describes being attracted to someone regardless of their biological sex or gender identity.

Passing: When someone is perceived as being a particular gender without others knowing they're trans. This is a controversial term because it suggests that the person is not truly what they're "passing" as.

Questioning: Describes someone who thinks they may not be cisgender, but hasn't quite figured things out 100 percent yet.

Sex: *see* Biological sex

Sexual orientation: Who you're attracted to.

Skoliosexual: Describes being primarily attracted to people who don't conform to the traditional gender binary.

Stealth: Living day-to-day life around people who don't know you're trans.

T: Testosterone.

Top surgery: The surgical removal or construction of breasts.

Transgender: Describes someone whose gender identity is different from the sex they were assigned at birth. The term is used as an adjective instead of a noun. Saying "a transgender" or "transgenders" as opposed to "transgender person" or "transgender people" can cause offense.

Transition: The period in which someone starts to live as the identity they feel a connection to. This can be made up of social or medical changes.

Transphobia: The dislike of or prejudice against transgender people.

RESOURCES

Trans culture

FTM Magazine
www.ftmmagazine.com
Trans masculine lifestyle magazine.

Hudson's FTM Resource Guide
www.ftmguide.org
Website filled with useful information on FTM topics.

Trans Guys
www.transguys.com
Magazine for transgender men.

Angels
www.angelsforum.co.uk/phpforum
Online forum for the transgender community.

Rights and Support

American Civil Liberties Union
www.aclu.org/know-your-rights/transgender-people-and-law
An organization that works to defend and preserve the individual
rights and liberties guaranteed by the Constitution and laws of the
United States.

National Center for Transgender Equality
www.transequality.org
A social justice advocacy organization that pushes the need for policy
change to advance transgender equality.

Human Rights Campaign
www.hrc.org/explore/topic/transgender
An organization that works to educate the public on issues that
transgender people face and to advocate for full inclusion and equality.

GLAAD
www.glaad.org/transgender/resources
A nongovernmental media-monitoring organization founded by LGBT
people in the media.

Alex Bertie

ALEX BERTIE

started making videos on sexuality and gender identity at age fourteen, and continues to do so today with weekly uploads to his hundreds of thousands of YouTube subscribers. His work has been picked up by organizations such as Childline and Stonewall, and has been recognized by the *Independent*, YouTube magazine *TenEighty*, and trans publication *FTM Magazine*. He lives in England and invites you to visit him on Twitter @Alex_Bertie, and on Instagram and YouTube @TheRealAlexBertie.